Grace
Faith
Works

Finding the Biblical Balance

Grace
Faith
Works

Finding the Biblical Balance

Larry M. Arrowood

Woodsong Publishing
Seymour, Indiana

GRACE FAITH WORKS: Finding the Biblical Balance

Larry M. Arrowood

Revised edition 2016

First Edition 1997 Prince of Peace Publishers

Woodsong Publishing
PO Box 863
Seymour, Indiana 47274

www.woodsongpublishing.com

Cover design by Matthew Arrowood at Vision Graphics
Printed in the United States of America.

ISBN 978-0-9892291-4-2

CONTENTS

Dedication
Preface

Chapters

Some Personal Thoughts

Dedication

To The Tabernacle church family in Seymour, Indiana. Your love for the Lord and your hunger for His Word motivated me to develop this manuscript. We have grown together along this journey and must continue to do so until our Lord completes His work within us.

Preface

In most subjects the pendulum of thought tends to swing to polar extremes. We see a neighbor's child fail and we are quick to condemn their liberal views of discipline or lack of personal parental consecration—the child was on the promiscuous side. In contrast, the unfortunate failure of our own child evokes excuses, rationalization, and empathy—it was a mistake. Parenting skills vary from being a strict disciplinarian to being the child's best friend, often vacillating in parenting styles from child number one to child number three. Don't most of us mellow somewhat with age, especially when grand-parenting?

Such is the case with the subject of this book. The pendulum of personal beliefs regarding the function of grace, faith, and works tends to swing to an extreme, either far right or far left, depending upon multiple variables. It is amazing how circumstances and life's stages affect this.

Waiting for circumstances or a stage in life to bring a balance in our Christian walk isn't necessarily the best process; too often it's late in coming. It is best to develop a biblically balanced Christian walk early in one's spiritual journey. I'm not speaking of compromising with sin; rather, I'm suggesting a more middle of the road approach to life that is based upon Scripture. One's natural inclinations, intellectual prowess, and emotional responses can often be deceptive. This is especially true in the area of this book's subject. The extremes lack "the-salt-of-the-earth" quality spoken of by Christ. The light set on a hill, that should welcome the wayfaring wanderer, is ablaze with danger or smoldering with apathy. Consider the extremes of grace, faith, and works. Grace to an extreme tolerates sin. Faith to an extreme promotes a religious humanism (Man is a god because he controls God by faith—he simply speaks the word of faith and God must obey.). Works to an extreme creates Pharisaic tendencies (self-righteousness and hypocrisy). The remedy for extremism is to find the biblical balance of grace, faith, and works in daily living. That is the motivation for this book, not to become the authoritative voice regarding how you must live, but to challenge extremes and offer direction in seeking a biblical balance. I do not consider myself the master of this subject; rather, I'm a fellow student, and I wanted to share my study with others, trusting that it will bless. Thanks for reading.

Larry Arrowood

Part I

GRACE

Chapter 1

THE RIGHT CHOICE

Grace, faith, and works. Which is most important? Does one trump the other two? Could all three be necessary in our spiritual journey? Are all three necessary to make it to heaven? Some say yes, while others say no, often with a slant toward an extreme and generally placing emphasis on a particular "pet" Scripture. The Bible places emphasis on all three subjects; therefore, it is imperative that we consider the Holy Scripture in its entirety. We must avoid the tendency toward extremism and the tendency to pick and choose from Scripture. Each of the subjects should have their proper purpose in our Christian life. Thus the subtitle of this book: *Finding The Biblical Balance.*

In our efforts to make sure God gets the credit for our salvation, many have oversimplified the biblical teaching of salvation through grace. This extreme is a Raggedy Ann mentality: we are all rag dolls that God carries around in His arms, with complete passivity on our part. This approach completely ignores a multitude of Scriptures that encourage, some even demanding, action in our Christian faith. I believe most Christians recognize God's grace has saved them, but too few balance grace with faith and works. Some have complicated the biblical directive to "work out your salvation with fear and trembling" to the point that they live in guilt over past failures that even God has forgotten, ever trying to earn forgiveness by doing enough good deeds to tip the scale. Still, we must not overlook the plethora of demands by Christ Himself, recorded in the Gospels, and the instructions of the Apostles scattered throughout the New Testament Epistles, in regards to righteous living. To find a proper balance, we must recognize the yoke of Christ is not for our bondage but for our benefit.

The extremes of grace include those whose views are liberal, the "grace lovers," and those whose views are legalistic, the "grace killers." The "grace killers" accuse the "grace lovers" of promoting a cheap grace that doesn't fully appreciate the price Christ paid. The "grace lovers" negate the need for any action on the part of the individual believer, except to acknowledge Christ as Savior. The "grace lovers" accuse the "grace killers" of trying to earn salvation by good works. The "grace killers" accuse the "grace lovers" as being unworthy of salvation due to unrighteous living. The "grace lovers" counter by referencing the Prophet Isaiah, "But we are all as an unclean thing, and all our righteousnesses are as filthy rags . . . " (Isaiah 64:6). The "grace killers" quickly quote from Paul's letter to the Corinthians, "Know ye not that the unrighteous shall not inherit the kingdom of God? Be not deceived: neither fornicators, nor idolaters, nor adulterers, nor effeminate, nor abusers of themselves with mankind" (I Corinthians 6:9), but then add a dozen rules for good measure.

Who's right? Who's wrong?

Could both be right but need a more complete biblical balance? If we do not understand grace, we may live under constant guilt. Some even abandon the faith out of hopelessness in pleasing God. Alternately, if we do not understand Christian discipline (works), we may well become irresponsible, disappointing, and nonproductive in the cause of Christ. We may become self-deceived regarding how Christ perceives us, thinking Him passive regarding Christian disciplines to the point that godly living is tossed to the wind. Finally, if we live apart from faith, we certainly displease God, for without faith the Scripture proclaims it impossible to please God. Still, if we possess faith but never act upon that faith—an element of works—we forfeit our Christian purpose: light and salt to a lost and deteriorating society.

Major problems arise when we teach grace, faith, and works as individual doctrines that cancel out each other, rather than viable teachings that all have a place in the Christian experience. Grace, in its initial act, is God's only means of giving to us salvation. In the ongoing process of the Christian life, grace works toward keeping us saved. Works have to do with our relationship with God and our fellow man once God has saved us. Our works are insufficient unless enabled through God's grace. Both grace and works must incorporate faith: "But without faith it is impossible to please him: for he that cometh to God must believe that he is, and that he is a rewarder of them that diligently seek him" (Hebrews 11:6).

If isolated, the subjects of grace, faith, and works bring misunderstanding and incompleteness. The purpose for this study is to help us better understand the importance of grace, faith, and works in our lives and how all three work together to make us both pleasing to Christ and fruitful in His Kingdom. All three have significance in our Christian experience. When we say we are saved by the grace of God, this should not cancel out the importance of the teaching of James regarding works: "What doth it profit, my brethren, though a man say he hath faith, and have not works? can faith save him?" (James 2:14). Likewise, when we teach from James' writings that faith is manifest by our good works, this does not contradict the teaching of Paul regarding salvation by grace: "For by grace are ye saved through faith; and that not of yourselves: it is the gift of God: Not of works, lest any man should boast" (Ephesians 2:8-9). James pounds home the point that good works are essential if one has true faith, but he also acknowledges Abraham's righteousness came through faith and not his good deeds: "And the scripture was fulfilled which saith, Abraham believed God, and it was imputed unto him for righteousness: and he was called the Friend of God," (James 2:23). Grace, faith, and works go together.

God's grace does not save every sinner, but every sinner that will be saved will be saved by God's grace. Though only God's grace saves us, that grace is activated in our lives through faith in Christ. Yet faith is more than acknowledging with words our belief in Christ; faith is an internal force that generates action.

In trying to define faith, I relate to the story about the fellow who fell off a cliff. As he plunged headlong to his death, by chance

3

he caught hold of a small tree growing from a cleft in a rock. As he frantically yelled for someone to rescue him from this deadly situation, a voice echoed back across the valley, "I'll save you if you trust me." With delight the man replied, "Oh, yes, I trust you. By the way, who are you?" The voice responded, "I'm God," whereupon the man exclaimed, "Oh, thank God it's you. Yes God, I trust you, so, please save me before I plunge into the rocks below." The voice replied, "If you trust me to save you, let go of the tree." After a long pause, a trembling and frantic voice broke the silence. "Is there anyone else out there?"

Faith is more than passive words; faith is a noun that represents something very real. In comparison, hate, as a noun, is a feeling of intense hostility. You know that you hate someone or something because of the intense emotions you experience. These emotions, if left unchecked, lead to actions of retaliation and sometimes violence. In contrast, many reduce faith to mere spoken words, but words alone can be deceptive, even false. To simply say, "I believe," without some intense inner emotion that perpetuates one to action is mere rhetoric. A genuine faith becomes an active force that demands a response. We go beyond mere words, to a response such as: "Because of my faith in the atoning acts of Christ through His death, burial, and resurrection, I identify with Christ's atoning act by a response. I die to my sins by repentance, I am buried with Him through baptism, and I resurrect a new man through the infilling of His Spirit. I will never be the same. I am forever changed and desire to please Him with my life." Such an experience of faith has less to do with words and more to do with the heart—the seat of our emotions, from which actions arise—which involves what James wrote about. We can call it active faith, or, like James, we can call it works. First and foremost it is God's grace that planned and carried out such a redemptive plan. Still, when we consider Scripture, even the grace of God takes something more—faith on our part—to be activated in our lives. Yet our faith does not save us; God's grace saves us. His sole act of redemptive death at Calvary is applied to our sins and pays our debt of sin. Still, grace does not save us apart from personal faith; further, we can prevent the grace of God through unbelief and disobedience.

How then does Paul say we are saved by grace and not by works? "Not by works of righteousness which we have done, but according to His mercy He saved us . . . " (Titus 3:5). Further, how can James say, "Ye see then how that by works a man is justified, and not by faith only" (James 2:24)? Aren't these contradictory statements? If so, who is right? And wrong? Could both be right? If so, how?

Paul emphasized that we are justified by faith. "Where is boasting then? It is excluded. By what law? of works? Nay: but by the law of faith. Therefore we conclude that a man is justified by faith without the deeds of the law" (Romans 3:27-28). Were James and Paul polarized in their teachings regarding this subject? Is one wrong? No. Both Paul and James are right. It is our interpretations of their writings that are incomplete and sometimes incorrect.

When we look at these subjects extensively, without isolating one, we see that grace, faith, and works are vital in the Christian experience. From the beginning to the end of our Christian experience, we are saved by the work of God's grace in our lives. From the beginning to the end of our Christian journey, we must have faith. From beginning to end, faith is never passive; rather, faith is always active. Of the examples in Scripture, believers always responded: they sacrificed, they built, they journeyed, or they reacted (Hebrews 11:4, 7, 23-31). From beginning to end, faith always demands obedience. "By faith Abraham, when he was called to go out into a place which he should after receive for an inheritance, obeyed; and he went out, not knowing whither he went" (Hebrews 11:8). We cannot have faith without obedience; faith without obedience places us in a state of rebellion against God, not in God's favor. We will not be obedient apart from faith. True, some obey out of fear instead of faith, but fear is a temporary motivator, and it looses its force over time. Even if we are obedient out of fear, such an act still incorporates faith in the Word of God: we believe there is a God who will punish us. Faith motivated by fear is a very impersonal relationship with Christ.

It is possible to abuse grace. The abuse of grace is likewise a very impersonal relationship with Christ. When we use grace to excuse sins instead of forgive sin, we operate in disobedience to God's Word. We dull our sense of guilt, and our actions challenge the Word of God that warns of the "lake of fire" for those who are disobedient to His Word. We challenge the warnings of Scripture (Revelation 21:8; II Peter 3:1-7) regarding sin to appease the carnal nature that controls our hearts. Grace becomes the crutch for carnality.

Good works never merit salvation: salvation is God's gift, not God's paycheck. No matter how good a life we live, it is not our works of righteousness that save us. These may well be indicative of our love for Christ and our sincere desire to please Him, but they do not bring salvation. Nor does our faith save us, for many a vowed sinner still believes in God and the redemptive work of Christ. We are saved only through God's redemptive grace enacted by our faith. Salvation is impossible apart from the work of Christ at Calvary. This saving grace is activated in an individual through faith. "For by grace are ye saved through faith . . . " (Ephesians 2:8). We'll talk about the manner of applying grace later in this book; further, we will view the necessity of Christ's command for the New Birth experience (John 3:5). For now, let's consider that the New Birth is not a passive event; it demands action on the part of the individual. And the grace of God, once applied, leads to righteous living. Paul settled this question in a letter to the Roman Christians. "What shall we say then? Shall we continue in sin, that grace may abound? God forbid. How shall we, that are dead to sin, live any longer therein?" (Romans 6:1-2).

The story of the brass serpent, erected by Moses during Israel's wilderness wandering, is a strange occurrence among a people who were demanded to reframe from idols; still, it served a unique purpose that is significant for us to consider. The brass serpent lifted up by Moses in the wilderness possessed no miraculous or medicinal means of healing those Israelites bitten by the poisonous serpents.

> And the people spake against God, and against Moses, Wherefore have ye brought us up out of Egypt to die in the wilderness? for there is no bread, neither is there any water; and our soul loatheth this light bread. And the LORD sent fiery serpents among the people, and they bit the people; and much people of Israel died. Therefore the people came to Moses, and said, We have sinned, for we have spoken against the LORD, and against thee; pray unto the LORD, that he take away the serpents from us. And Moses prayed for the people. And the LORD said unto Moses, Make thee a fiery serpent, and set it upon a pole: and it shall

come to pass, that every one that is bitten, when he looketh upon it, shall live. And Moses made a serpent of brass, and put it upon a pole, and it came to pass, that if a serpent had bitten any man, when he beheld the serpent of brass, he lived.

Numbers 21:5-9

Not one of those snake-bitten victims was healed by the metallic image of a snake; conversely, it was God's mercy that healed them. However, the dying individual had to look upon the brass serpent, an act of obedience, before God healed them. Yet it was not their obedience that spared their lives, it was God's mercy. Still, had they not been obedient through faith (We are not sure how much faith was involved, for that was a quality the Israelites coming out of Egypt seemed to lack in multiple situations.), the grace of God would not have spared them, and I dare say some probably died because they refused to follow the plan for healing. Likewise, when we look with obedient faith to Christ, who was lifted up on the cross, God's grace is enacted in our lives and brings us salvation. Jesus explained that the brass serpent was a type of Calvary, which was to come. Jesus said: "And as Moses lifted up the serpent in the wilderness, even so must the Son of man be lifted up: That whosoever believeth in him should not perish, but have eternal life" (John 3:14-15).

In every example of conversion in Scripture there is always some demand and some act of obedience that enacts Christ's plan for redemption. Consider the conversions at the birth of the New Testament church: "Now when they heard this, they were pricked in their heart, and said unto Peter and to the rest of the apostles, Men and brethren, what shall we do? Then Peter said unto them, Repent, and be baptized every one of you in the name of Jesus Christ for the remission of sins, and ye shall receive the gift of the Holy Ghost" (Acts 2:37-38). Just like the first church believers, our obedience to Scripture enacts God's grace in our lives. We understand from whom and where salvation comes—God and His grace—but not apart from faith and obedience on our part. Obedient faith activates grace; lack of faith and acts of disobedience to Scriptural directives prevent the flow of grace in our lives. In the example of the first church converts, the acts of repentance and submission to water baptism were manifestations of obedient faith, which brought God's saving grace into their lives. This pattern was followed in subsequent conversions recorded in Scripture: the Samaritans, Acts 8:12-17; Paul, Acts 9:17-19; the Gentiles, Acts 10:44-48; disciples of John the Baptist, Acts 19:1-6. We should expect no lesser acts of obedient faith than these. God's affirmative gift to those obedient believers was the Holy Spirit baptism as was explained to Nicodemus by Jesus (John 3:1-5). We respond with obedient faith, and God responds by bestowing salvation. It is extremely important we not confuse faith with positive thinking, or emotional hype. Faith is not a mental game; it has tangible evidence: "Faith is the substance . . . the evidence . . . " (Hebrews 11:1). The basis for our faith is not "pie in the sky;" the basis for our faith is God's Word. What God has spoken through Scripture is the bedrock for building faith.

Therefore, in viewing the host of references, let us explore each of these subjects: grace, faith, and works. Further, let us work toward understanding the biblical balance of all three. Let us not allow any one topic to cancel out the need for the other in our Christian walk; rather, let us allow each their proper place within our lives. The grace of God comes first: it awakens faith within our hearts. "For the grace of God that bringeth salvation hath appeared to all men, teaching us that, denying ungodliness and worldly lusts, we should live soberly, righteously, and godly, in this present world" (Titus 2:11,12). As we consider God's grace, our faith increases and causes us to look to God for salvation. This leads us to the New Birth experience as demanded by Christ, where God's grace is activated within our hearts, expanding our faith, and ultimately producing the works of righteousness in our lives. It is extremely important that each of these are in proper order: grace activates faith; faith leads us to the salvation experience; works of righteousness are the result of the living Savior within us.

If we have experienced salvation, it is only by God's grace, but this did not happen apart from faith that allowed us to believe God for salvation and motivated us to seek such through obedience to Scripture. There's no example in Scripture of anyone getting saved on their terms: all followed a plan of God, which is consistent throughout Scripture. Further, if we loose our faith, we abandon our reliance upon God's grace, and ultimate miserably fail God, sometimes digressing into self-righteousness and living in deception. If we purposefully walk in disobedience to Scripture, we mock God's grace. Yet, the best that we could ever be does not make us good enough for heaven—grace does. We'll make it to heaven by His grace, not by our good works. In the meantime, we should live as pleasing to Him as possible, ever aligning our lives with the Scripture. This takes effort on our part, but we are not alone in the challenge: we have the empowering Holy Spirit resident within.

Some may perceive a quest for what pleases God as embracing legalism, but that is not the case. Legalism is trying to merit salvation. Pursuit of God and His righteousness is a life motivated by the indwelling Savior. Anyone who is not pursuing the righteousness of God is not being lead of the Holy Spirit. We understand that to stop sinning and start doing good deeds still does not qualify a person for heaven, but grace—having been activated in one's life—does. How? Grace says, "Christ's sacrifice on Calvary paid his/her debt of sin." Case closed. But grace doesn't just leave us where it found us; grace brings a desire to stop sinning. However, our lack of sinning does not save us: the grace of God saves us. As grace works in our lives, sin no longer dominates. We receive continuing grace to put off the works of darkness and put on the works of righteousness (an almost forgotten simple Christian principle of doing that which is good and stop doing that which is bad). If we sin, grace is present to lead us to repentance, and Christ forgives our sins. The process motivates us to "sin no more" as Jesus commanded the adulteress. Indeed, this seems a bit old fashioned for some modern Christians who've been taught grace is our license to sin. We'll discuss this later in chapter six, but the point we need to understand before we attempt to live for Christ is this, salvation " . . . is the gift of God" (Ephesians 2:8); it's not something we earn. We do not receive this gift until we recognize that we are hopelessly lost—though children are capable of giving their lives to Christ before they fully comprehend sin and its effects. No amount of personal goodness can earn salvation. Many of us have tried, and for a while we may have been pleased with the results, but somewhere along the way we saw ourselves alongside the Holy God, and the picture of ourselves was not good. We must keep coming back to the bedrock of our salvation: Jesus Christ and Him crucified. And once here, we receive forgiveness, faith, desire, and strength to go on, recognizing that not only did Christ begin the work of salvation in us, He is the one that continues the work and ultimately will finish the work. "For we are his workmanship, created in Christ Jesus unto good works, which God hath before ordained that we should walk in them" (Ephesians 2:10). To experience this is to have a biblical balance of grace, faith, and works—constant companions for the Christian journey—which work in harmony and not in contention.

To pursue salvation apart from grace is a journey destined for failure; at best it leaves us with gnawing guilt, and at worst it leads us into a state of self-righteousness: proud, arrogant, and critical of others who do not measure up to our standards of commitment, discipline, and obedience to a list of rules. How strange, for Jesus called those of his day—who held to this believe and practice—hypocrites! Christ well knew that no one can be holy apart from grace, and no one can continually produce the works of righteousness apart from the works of grace, and the self-righteous attitude of the Pharisees was void of grace.

The guilt associated with sin can only be removed by a realization of the sin and an experience of the grace of God, which removes the sins. Jesus did not condemn the Pharisees because they pursued righteous living; conversely, He is our greatest example of righteousness. He condemned them because of their arrogance. They felt their perceived right living merited heaven.

Grace and good works are not at war with each other, neither tallying up the points scored. Good works are the result of vigorous effort for some, but for a Christian, it is the result of vigorous effort motivated and aided by the sanctifying process of grace—a journey of holiness. A lack of personal commitment in the journey of holiness hinders the work of grace, bordering closer and closer to the area of disobedience, which prevents the work of grace. And our faith, once sharpened by the whet rock of God's stroking grace, becomes dull and insensitive to the actions that please Christ. The Christian journey becomes a drudgery, or boring, or too long. We become careless, driving daringly too close to the precipice of Satan's deception, and we allow the desire for the world to dominate our decisions.

Jerry Bridges, author of numerous books on this subject, expresses so superbly this balance when he writes:

> The Holy Spirit's work in transforming us more and more into the likeness of Christ is called sanctification. Our involvement and cooperation with Him in His work is what I call the pursuit of holiness.
>
> The pursuit of holiness requires sustained and vigorous effort. It allows for no indolence, no lethargy, no halfhearted commitment, and no laissez faire attitude toward even the smallest sins. In short, it demands the highest priority in the life of a Christian, because to be holy is to be like Christ—God's goal for every Christian.
>
> At the same time, however, the pursuit of holiness must be anchored in the grace of God; otherwise it is doomed to failure. That statement probably strikes many people as strange. A lot of Christians seem to think that the grace of God and the vigorous pursuit of holiness are antithetical—that is, in direct and unequivocal opposition to one another.
>
> To some, the pursuit of holiness sounds like legalism and manmade rules. To others, an emphasis on grace seems to open the door to irresponsible, sinful behavior based on the notion that God's unconditional love means we are free to sin as we please.
>
> Grace and the personal discipline required to pursue holiness, however, are not opposed to one another. In fact, they go hand in hand. An understanding of how grace and personal, vigorous effort work together is essential for a life-long pursuit of holiness. Yet many believers do not understand what it means to live by grace in their daily lives, and they certainly don't understand the relationship of grace to personal discipline."[1]

Grace, faith, and works properly balanced lead us on a journey with Christ. On this journey, Christ walks, talks, and shares with us His forgiveness, His love, His will, and His ways. We listen, we learn, we labor. He never leaves us alone on this journey, " . . . for he hath said, I will never leave thee, nor forsake thee" (Hebrews 13:5). We dare not leave Him; rather, we need to continually pursue to " . . . walk in the Spirit . . . " (Galatians 5:16). I've heard it said of this Christian walk, "It's a life long journey, not a week-end trip." A word in the Bible that keeps leaping out at me is "continue." The word is key in our journey. We must not linger on this journey, but we must continue. And our luggage? You guessed it. Let's take with us God's amazing grace, ample faith, and works worthy of our title: a child of God.

Chapter 2

GRACE EXAMINED

Let's examine grace.

Some years ago when my teenage son Andrew ran a red light, his experience brought to light the meaning of grace. Fortunately, no other vehicles came through the intersection at the same time; unfortunately for him, a city policeman observed the entire scenario. The ensuing conversation went something like this:

Officer: "Can I see your drivers license?"

Andrew: "Sure. Uh, I'm sorry, officer."

Officer: (He studied the driver's license.) "What's your dad's name?"

Andrew: "Larry Arrowood."

Officer: "Is he the pastor of the church uptown?"

Andrew: "Yes, sir."

Officer: "What would you say if I just rip you some and let you go?"

Andrew: "Start ripping!"

Guilty? Yes. Could he change the fact that he ran the red light? Absolutely not. Did he deserve a ticket? The law said yes. Further, to stop at ten thousand red lights would not change the fact that he ran one. To obey all traffic rules the rest of his life does not erase the one violation. Andrew could not undo, nor redo. But the officer made the decision not to charge him. Grace! Unmerited favor. The question remains, with a policeman showing favors, should he continue to run red lights? The answer is obvious.

Grace stands alone. It does not need to be propped up by good works. Grace is about God and His love and goodness, not about who or what we are. Christ died for our debt of sin, extending grace, while we were yet in our sins. If good works could save us, Christ died needlessly.

Why did Christ die for our sins? Was it pity? Was it manipulation? Was it a ploy? No. It was His love for a fallen creation. We were in a mess from which we had no means to escape. We had drifted beyond the point of no return. We owed a debt, which we could never pay. Christ died specifically to pay the debt of the sins of mankind. Calvary extended grace for all. Grace does not just pardon or excuse sins, grace pays the debt accrued by our sins. When we are baptized ("buried with Christ" is the biblical phraseology), Christ's atoning blood is applied to our sins—it's as if we died to pay for our sins. We are free from the debt of sin, for the debt is considered by God as paid in full.

Why the need for grace? An attribute of God, justice, demanded that man's sins be paid for—not just excused. Prior to mankind's failure in the garden, God established the rules regarding sin: "And the Lord God commanded the man, saying, Of every tree of the garden thou mayest freely eat: But of the tree of the knowledge of good and evil, thou shalt not eat of it: for in the day that thou eatest thereof thou shalt surely die" (Genesis 2:16-17). The New Testament reflects the same theme regarding sin: "For the wages of sin is death . . . " (Romans 6:23). Since God's attribute bound Him to justice, He designed a plan whereby He paid our debt by His own death. Though sinless, Christ submitted to a cruel death, thus satisfying the punishment that justice demanded for sin. The price paid for mankind's redemption cost God greatly.

Does God's plan for redemption mean that all of mankind will be saved? Absolutely not, but it means that all mankind has a means of salvation. "For God so loved the world, that he gave his only begotten Son, that whosoever believeth in him should not perish, but have everlasting life" (John 3:16). The means to salvation is revealed in Scripture, but also the seriousness of sin: "And if the righteous scarcely be saved, where shall the ungodly and the sinner appear?" (I Peter 4:18). The basic difference between sinners and saints is the applied grace of God: "All have sinned and come short of the glory of God" (Romans 3:23). Has God then shown favoritism, giving grace to a select few? No. His death brought grace to all mankind, but mankind must accept it individually. Otherwise, all people—Atheists, Agnostics, Hitler, Jim Jones—no matter how they lived, would automatically be saved. The Scripture is quite alarming regarding God's stringency concerning salvation: the lost will far outweigh the saved. "Enter ye in at the strait gate: for wide is the gate, and broad is the way, that leadeth to destruction, and many there be which go in thereat: Because strait is the gate, and narrow is the way, which leadeth unto life, and few there be that find it" (Matthew 7:13-14).

To whom then is grace applied? The playing field quickly narrows, for grace is extended to those who believe on Christ. Who are those who believe on Christ? The true believers are those who obey His Word. John emphasizes obedience in his letter to the church:

> My little children, these things write I unto you, that ye sin not. And if any man sin, we have an advocate with the Father, Jesus Christ the righteous: And he is the propitiation for our sins: and not for ours only, but also for the sins of the whole world. And hereby we do know that we know him if we keep his commandments. He that saith, I know him, and keepeth not his commandments, is a liar, and the truth is not in him. But whoso keepeth his word, in him verily is the love of God perfected: hereby know we that we

15

are in him. He that saith he abideth in him ought himself also so to walk, even as he walked. Brethren, I write no new commandment unto you, but an old commandment which ye had from the beginning. The old commandment is the word which ye have heard from the beginning.

1 John 2:1-7

Aren't we back to grace needing works to prop it up? No, for if grace needs works to make it sufficient to save us, then it is not grace, for grace is unearned. If man had not failed God in the beginning, we would not be separated from God, so there would have been no need for grace. Once man sinned, his sin brought separation, and sin doomed mankind to forever be cast out of God's presence. No matter how good one may have lived, he was still lost in his sin, eternally separated from God. To understand this, let's consider the factors that existed in the creation of man.

The first consideration, though man was created perfect, he had the ability to choose to love and obey God, or reject and disobey God. Adam and Eve were not mere puppets controlled by their creator. They were created with a mind to think and a will to choose.

The second consideration, God planted within the garden two trees: the tree of life and the tree of the knowledge of good and evil. It is difficult for us to comprehend what these two trees were like, so it is best to simply take the Scripture at face value: one represented obedience, the other disobedience. God commanded man to abstain from the tree of the knowledge of good and evil, and He warned of the consequences of disobedience: both a physical and a spiritual death (Genesis 2:9, 16-17). Since man had never experienced death, this warning had to be accepted by faith in God's good character and His authority as Creator. Adam and Eve had to believe that God was good, was on their side, and looked out for their interest. This was not without tangible evidence, for God communed often with them, Creator to creation. We must consider that they had everything they needed, but greed entered the picture and they wanted more.

The third consideration is the role Satan played. As the adversary of God, he tempted Adam and Eve to disbelieve and disobey God (Genesis 3:1-5). Through subtlety Satan convinced them their creator had flaws, withheld some good from them, and if they followed his direction they could actually be God's equal. No longer would they be renters, they would be landowners, sharing in the bounty. There's no indication Adam and Eve ever communicated with God regarding Satan's lies. They assumed the worst about God and believed the lies of Satan, assuming he had their true interest. The rest is a tragic account. "And when the woman saw that the tree was good for food, and that it was pleasant to the eyes, and a tree to be desired to make one wise, she took of the fruit thereof, and did eat, and gave also unto her husband with her; and he did eat" (Genesis 3:6).

The fourth consideration is mankind's fallen state. Once Adam and Eve ate of the forbidden tree, they lost their perfection, tainted by disbelief, selfishness, and disobedience, a category into which all sin can be classified. "And the eyes of them both were opened, and they knew that they were naked; and they sewed fig leaves together, and made themselves aprons" (Genesis 3:7). Humankind found itself in an immediate state of separation from God (Genesis 3:8, 23-24). They had no means to bridge the chasm of separation. They chose this fate by obeying Satan. This wasn't done in ignorance; it was a calculated choice. Sin compromised their perfect nature; ultimately, sin alienated them from God. God did not hide from them; their sinful nature caused them to hide from God. God came looking for them. Spiritual death occurred immediately: the breathe of God ceased to permeate their being and carnality surged throughout their spirit.

Man did not immediately die physically; rather, the process of death began. God read the verdict of guilt, announced the punishment, and drove them from the garden. They were banished from God's presence. At the same time, God set in motion a plan—designed from the creation of the world—to redeem fallen man back to Himself. God extended grace instead of eternal damnation. It was a bold plan, conceived out of the love of God for His creation: " . . . the Lamb slain from the foundation of the world" (Revelation 13:8).

The fifth consideration is this grace that God extended. Though punished and banished from God's presence, in the same courtroom of justice, God promised redemption. Satan was exposed as God's enemy, and the serpent, which Satan embodied to beguile Eve, was punished severely, but within that proclamation of punishment is the first glimpse of grace: "And I will put enmity between thee and the woman, and between thy seed and her seed; it shall bruise thy head, and thou shalt bruise his heel" (Genesis 3:15). God's grace made redemption possible for mankind. It wasn't extended to Satan. Nor does it automatically blanket the whole of mankind. God extended grace even before the fall. Some four thousand years later the prophet John revealed the sacrificial Lamb of God, conceived before mankind's existence. The thundering prophet proclaimed, " . . . Behold the Lamb of God, which taketh away the sin of the world. This is he of whom I said, After me cometh a man which is preferred before me: for he was before me" (John 1:29-30).

First, grace emanated from the heart of God; it was not a result of mankind seeking God. Grace was not pity (though fallen mankind was a pitiful plight); rather, grace was an extension of Who God is. Because of God's great love for His creation, He extended grace to all mankind. Grace is activated individually as mankind seeks God. The quest for God began soon after the fall (Genesis 4:26; 6:5-9; 12:1-4). Thus, when we consider grace, we must discuss three areas: what grace is, how grace is applied, and to whom grace is applied.

What is grace? It is the unmerited favor of God. The awesome Creator God wasn't obligated in any way to save a human race kicking Him on the shin and choosing to follow Satan, God's avowed archenemy. Mankind was without excuse, for he didn't have to sin. His originally created nature wasn't carnal; rather, it was like God's nature, free of sin. Sin was mankind's personal choice. After the fall, mankind didn't deserve nor request grace, nor was he able to attain it on his own, but God made it available. "While we were yet sinners, Christ died . . . " (Romans 5:8). Christ's death at Calvary released grace to past, present, and future generations.

How is this unmerited favor applied? Depending upon the timeline of one's existence, God imparted grace to many in various circumstances: Noah (who tried to live righteous in an unrighteous world—though his righteousness was obviously flawed, or else he would not have become drunken); Abraham (faith and obedience to God's call of separation—though he acquiesced to his fears on more than one occasion); Israel (the covenant agreement, including the sacrificial system—the system basically postponed judgment and served to show how sinful mortal man truly is); Jonah (repentance and submission to God's will—though interrupted by rebellion and pouting); David (a prayer of acknowledgement of sin and deep repentance—under the Mosaic Law he should have been stoned). From the birth of the church until the present, Jesus proclaimed our entrance into God's kingdom (where grace abounds) is through the New Birth experience, not our personal goodness. "Jesus answered and said unto him, Verily, verily, I say unto thee, Except a man be born again, he cannot see the kingdom of God" (John 3:3). All of these examples of extended grace to mortal man were made possible through Christ's death as our sacrificial lamb. Some received grace before Christ died. How? In God's omniscience He recognized the future event of Calvary and thus released grace into the lives of those who sought Him, even before Christ's death. In retrospect, we receive grace because Christ died. His past death releases grace to us in the present. The grace released at Calvary flows both backwards (to those of the Old Testament) and forwards (to our present generation). Had not Christ died, grace would never have been extended to mortal man.

To whom is grace applied? All receive a measure of grace, else we would fall into judgment. Still, the dispensing of grace is on an individual basis, not a blanket application. It is applied to those individuals who accept it through obedient faith. Grace continues to be applied as we allow Jesus to be Lord of our lives. Grace applied is both the act of a single event—a specific time when it comes to a life at Christian conversion—but also a continuing process as we walk with the Lord Jesus.

The first act of grace calls us to accept Christ's substitute sacrifice for our sins. Our response in obedient faith to God's written Word enacts saving grace within our lives. Each example of conversion in Scripture offers specific acts on the part of the believer, including: a repentant heart, water and Spirit baptism, and a continuance in God. These were consistent for the Jewish believers (Acts 2), the Samaritan believers (Acts 8), the Gentile believers (Acts 10), and the followers of John the Baptist (Acts 19). All sought God diligently with a repentant heart, were baptized into Christ (The specific name of the Savior was applied at baptism, in contrast to a later baptismal formula which omits the actual name of the Savior and substitutes His title as son.), and experienced the Holy Spirit infilling. Finally, grace keeps us in Christ even though we live in the midst of an evil and alluring worldly system. "But grow in grace, and in the knowledge of our Lord and Saviour Jesus Christ . . . " (II Peter 3:18).

The overall act of grace (Biblical terms include: justification, sanctification, transformation, redemption) has three recognizable segments. The initial act of grace culminates in the New Birth experience explained by Christ to the searching Nicodemus (John 3:1-7). This initial segment includes both the removal of our sinful garments and the re-clothing with God's garments of righteousness. Our unrighteousness is removed (through repentance and water baptism into Christ), and we are re-clothed with His righteousness through Holy Spirit baptism. Recognize the essentiality of the New Birth, for there can be no spiritual transformation without the spiritual death of the old man and the rebirth of a new man. Some call this initial segment sanctification.

The second segment of grace is a continual sanctification. The grace of Christ is applied in our lives day by day. And God, who is " . . . merciful and gracious, slow to anger, and plenteous in mercy" (Psalms 103:8), directs our lives daily. We find grace to bear, grace to change, grace to overcome, grace to forgive, and grace that offers forgivness. Our love for Christ and appreciation for His atoning work at Calvary causes us to aggressively and continually seek His face, study His Word, and serve His purpose. We have nothing to boast of save Christ's saving grace, for we understand our previous condition. We understand that our present state of worthiness still rests upon His continual grace working in our lives, for we cannot attain righteousness on our own merit. As we grow in grace and knowledge of Christ, we become keener to those things that displease Him. We become quick to repent of such sins and less prone to repeat them. "For sin shall not have dominion over you . . . " (Romans 6:14). We aggressively seek to cast off the sins and weights that so easily beset us (Hebrews 12:1). It is here that we never sink so low that Christ's grace cannot catch us, nor rise too high that we no longer depend upon His grace. We also realize that we should seek to "walk worthy" of the grace of God (Ephesians 4:1, Colossians 1:10, I Thessalonians 2:12). We seek to acquire biblical disciplines, and we allow the indwelling Spirit and the instruction of Scripture to become our constant guide.

Those that experience initial grace, and continue in the same, will eventually partake of the third segment of grace, termed "ultimate sanctification." This takes place at the rapture. Our journey will be completed; grace will have done its perfect work. Until that day, grace is applied through faith in the atoning sacrifice of Christ. Consider a word of caution: faith is never passive. Faith is much more than verbalization, though that is a part. Faith is obedience in action. The most noted Bible characters of faith were characterized by their action: Noah built an Ark; Abraham left his homeland and followed God; David slew Goliath. In comparison to how we sometimes identify faith, King Saul could be considered the one having faith as he sat in his tent waiting on God to take care of the giant. Conversely, David, the lad of action, represented faith. Instead of passivity, faith motivates and inspires one to action and obedience to God's Word.

It would be comforting—though tragic—for us to assume the position that God's grace is so awesome it automatically covers everyone. After all, doesn't everyone have a good side? Such philosophy suggests the entire world will be saved: all because of grace. The Scripture is too brutally clear to give consideration to such thoughts. We have no right to paint a distorted picture of God as Mr. Nice, neglecting the scriptural concept of His hatred for sin, and His judicial obligation and warning that He will judge sin. God is neither Mr. Nice Guy nor Mr. Bad Guy; rather, He is the creator of all that exists and the judge of all He has created. He offers grace to cover sin; however, even His grace will not stop the final judgment of God of those who have rejected His grace. All mankind will be judged, for the Scripture proclaims, " . . . for we shall all stand before the judgment seat of Christ" (Romans 14:10). There seems to be a distinction between the "judgment seat of Christ" and the "great white throne judgment" (Revelation 20:11-15). Between these two judgments, every individual (righteous and wicked) will give an account for the life he has lived. The redeemed will appear before the judgment seat of Christ immediately after the rapture; all others will appear at the great white throne judgment immediately after the millennial reign. God's applied grace, made possible by the atoning blood of Christ, covers the debt of sin of born again believers. All who are not covered by grace will be judged guilty of sin at the great white throne judgment. Those who have rejected the grace of God will still owe their debt of sin.

> And I saw a great white throne, and him that sat on it, from whose face the earth and the heaven fled away; and there was found no place for them. And I saw the dead, small and great, stand before God; and the books were opened: and another book was opened, which is the book of life: and the dead were judged out of those things which were written in the books, according to their works. And the sea gave up the dead which were in it; and death and hell delivered up the dead which were in them: and they were judged every man according to their works. And death and hell were cast into the lake of fire. This is the second death. And whosoever was not found written in the book of life was cast into the lake of fire.
>
> Revelation 20:11-15

God gave grace, but He does not force grace upon anyone. He made provision for salvation for all, yet He created man-kind with a free will to choose or reject this salvation., made provision for salvation for all, yet He created mankind with a free will to choose or reject this salvation. All in Noah's day had opportunity to be saved; unfortunately, all but eight people refused to enter the ark and therefore drowned in the flood. Was not all of Lot's family invited to escape God's wrath on Sodom? Nevertheless, only Lot, his wife, and two daughters accepted God's mercy and fled the city. Even still, Lot's wife looked back and turned into a pillar of salt. Evidently her heart remained in Sodom, perhaps because of her children left behind. But she rejected provision for redemption. Salvation is always a personal choice.

Some argue that we're now under the grace of the New Testament and not under the curse of the Old Testament Law. Since we're under grace, many suggest we don't have to view sin so seriously. Consider that our examples, Noah and Lot, preceded the giving of the Law. Even without the written Law of Moses, mankind was held responsible for sin. Prior to the Law, God's innate law governed mankind. In both of the above examples, some were saved, and some were lost. Punishment for sin was not isolated to the era of the Law. God has always shown to mankind a standard of righteousness for which he is responsible. Throughout the Old Testament and concluding in the final book of the New Testament, some are lost and some are saved, but mankind was never without a means of grace. There is no more grace after Calvary than there was before Calvary; the difference is that we know the source of grace: Calvary. After Calvary we are allowed a greater intimacy with God because of our keener knowledge of His Word and the personal baptism of the Spirit, but God's grace has abounded since the creation. Because Calvary would happen, God was able to extend grace to those of the Old Testament; further, because Calvary has happened, God extends grace to us. The point? Grace is God's unmerited favor to us because of His sacrifice at Calvary, not because anyone is uniquely special. After we've accepted grace, we're uniquely special; still, we owe everything to Christ. "For by grace are ye saved through faith; and that not of yourselves: it is the gift of God: Not of works, lest any man should boast. For we are his workmanship, created in Christ Jesus unto good works, which God hath before ordained that we should walk in them" (Ephesians 2:8-10).

Even the angels of heaven did not fully comprehend the Incarnation, how God became man to ransom a fallen creation. "Unto whom it was revealed, that not unto themselves, but unto us they did minister the things, which are now reported unto you by them that have preached the gospel unto you with the Holy Ghost sent down from heaven; which things the angels desire to look into" (I Peter 1:12). The prophets inquired into the source of grace, how the slaying of an animal could spare the judgment of God upon mortals, but they could never fully comprehend what God had in mind at Calvary. "Of which salvation the prophets have enquired and searched diligently, who prophesied of the grace that should come unto you" (I Peter 1:10). The psalmist David had some insight, and under the inspiration of the Spirit, wrote prophetically regarding the Messiah (Psalm 22). The Prophet Isaiah described the Incarnation and crucifixion, probably without full comprehension of what and how God intended to extend grace.

23

Who hath believed our report? and to whom is the arm of the LORD revealed? For he shall grow up before him as a tender plant, and as a root out of a dry ground: he hath no form nor comeliness; and when we shall see him, there is no beauty that we should desire him. He is despised and rejected of men; a man of sorrows, and acquainted with grief: and we hid as it were our faces from him; he was despised, and we esteemed him not. Surely he hath borne our griefs, and carried our sorrows: yet we did esteem him stricken, smitten of God, and afflicted. But he was wounded for our transgressions, he was bruised for our iniquities: the chastisement of our peace was upon him; and with his stripes we are healed. All we like sheep have gone astray; we have turned every one to his own way; and the LORD hath laid on him the iniquity of us all. He was oppressed, and he was afflicted, yet he opened not his mouth: he is brought as a lamb to the slaughter, and as a sheep before her shearers is dumb, so he openeth not his mouth. He was taken from prison and from judgment: and who shall declare his generation? for he was cut off out of the land of the living: for the transgression of my people was he stricken. And he made his grave with the wicked, and with the rich in his death; because he had done no violence, neither was any deceit in his mouth.

Psalm 53:1-9

Calvary was not an afterthought God came up with after the Law proved insufficient. Calvary was God's visible manifestation of His grace toward us even before we sinned. "And all that dwell upon the earth shall worship him, whose names are not written in the book of life of the Lamb slain from the foundation of the world" (Revelation 13:8). Calvary was a plan to enact grace in a manner that would satisfy God's attributes of holiness and mercy. Holiness and mercy are a part of the divine attributes that form the nature of God. God's holiness separates Him from mankind; God's mercy draws Him to mankind. Both attributes existed before the creation of man, they are what God is and will always be. Mankind's sin placed these attributes in conflict; Calvary satisfied both, the result being that God could extend grace to a fallen creation. Calvary was God's ultimate manifestation of His love; further, it was the ultimate manifestation of punishment for sin—the sinless Christ suffered the guilt and shame of all sinners. No other acts of God's grace to mankind match the love manifest on a hill called Golgotha. How can we reject such love? And such love existed in the beginning, for God knew that mankind would fail, but He created a plan whereby He would die for His creation. The plan's sole motivation was God's love: "For God so loved the world, that he gave his only begotten Son, that whosoever believeth in him should not perish, but have everlasting life" (John 3:16).

God's grace remained throughout man's existence but always pointed toward Christ's sacrifice. Perhaps the first example was God slaying an animal and symbolically clothing Adam and Eve with the skin of the slain animal. This sacrifice had its authority, not just in the fact that God slew the animal and covered Adam and Eve, but its source of authority was its anticipation of Calvary. Even the Law, with all its goriness of animal sacrifices and minute regulations, was a part of the work of grace, in that it showed us we were sinners in need of a savior. All of creation inherited the sinful nature of Adam and ultimately act upon that sinful nature. Just as all inherit their sinful nature from one man, all receive access to God's grace through one man, Jesus Christ. God looks to no other source to extend grace except to Christ's sacrificial death.

> For scarcely for a righteous man will one die: yet peradventure for a good man some would even dare to die. But God commendeth his love toward us, in that, while we were yet sinners, Christ died for us. Much more than, being now justified by his blood, we shall be saved from wrath through him. For if, when we were enemies, we were reconciled to God by the death of his Son, much more, being reconciled, we shall be saved by his life. And not only so, but

we also joy in God through our Lord Jesus Christ, by whom we have now received the atonement. Wherefore, as by one man sin entered into the world, and death by sin; and so death passed upon all men, for that all have sinned: For until the law sin was in the world: but sin is not imputed when there is no law. Nevertheless death reigned from Adam to Moses, even over them that had not sinned after the similitude of Adam's transgression, who is the figure of him that was to come.

Romans 5:7-14

The Law was not just some nasty trick God played on Israel. It served a distinct and important role in bringing mankind to a redemptive state from the Fall. Though it consisted of a lot of symbolic ceremonies, it also shared the ethical and moral principles of God, principles that never change. These principles were to be applied not only to the people of Israel, but they are applicable still to all that love God. When Christ came, He did not come to do away with these ethical and moral laws. He came to explain and to show us by example how to live. Portions of the Law were symbolic of some greater godly truth, thus we no longer partake of the symbolism, but we look to that which it represents. We'll cover later in this book some of those symbols and how we are to adapt some into the Christian faith.

Mankind rejected God's grace and plunged headlong into moral decay and idolatry. In order to preserve His creation, God called Abraham to produce a lineage committed to maintaining the principles of morality and monotheism. Abraham's descendants entered into a covenant relationship with God to obey the Law given at Sinai. It was this Law that established a benchmark of separation of the expectations of God versus a depraved society. Consider then, without the Law, the creation could have remained in debauchery, unaware of its state of depravity. This was the situation in Noah's day (Genesis 6:1-5), to the point that God destroyed the world with a flood. Rather than repeat this action of judgment every few generations, God chose a people to whom He gave personal attention and specific guidelines on how they should live. The Law of God at Sinai allowed mankind to view himself apart from God and eternally lost and needing a means of redemption. The Law at Sinai and the recorded words of the prophets representing God became the rulebook from which God judged mankind. These teachings of the Law, along with recorded history, songs and prayers, and the proclamations of the prophets formulated what we call the Old Testament; ultimately, the Old Testament represented not just those things that were morally right or wrong, but it represented the authority of God—God is in charge of His universe. Whether we understand the rules or not, God is in command of the creation. There was nothing inherently wrong in picking up sticks on the Sabbath, but when God said don't pick up sticks on the Sabbath, He meant for man not to pick up sticks on the Sabbath. Why? I could offer a hosts of reasons, but the best reason is simply because God said so. To reject His authority is rebellion.

There's an interesting account in the Scripture (I Kings 13) where God gave command to a prophet to deliver a message. The command also included directions regarding what route the prophet should take and where he should eat. Somehow the prophet rationalized regarding what he evidently considered insignificant details. The consequences? He was killed by a lion. Why? He disregarded the authority of God. Jerry Bridges writes of this account:

> "That God would use such a word in this instance is all the more striking because the prophet who defied God didn't commit a scandalous sin. He simply did what God had specifically told him not to do—to eat or drink in the land of Samaria or return by the way he came. Yet God regarded his sin not as mere disobedience on the level we associate with that word but as defiance. Again, the seriousness of sin is not simply measured by its consequences, but by the authority of the One who gives the command."[1]

We read accounts such as this, or of someone being killed for picking up sticks on the Sabbath, and we don't quite comprehend why the punishment was so severe. We are certainly glad we don't live under those circumstances. Because of the awesome message of grace, we breathe a sign of relief—and spend the Sabbath at Walmart picking through the sales items. However, in our interpreting the message of grace, we often overlook a principle of God that has never changed: He is still in charge. His Word is still His authority. Though He has covered our sins at Calvary, we are not excused to live spiritually sloppy and to disregard His Word. We need to recognize that grace does not ignore godly directives of Scripture. We need to consider that the moral laws of God, and the principles of righteousness established by both the Old and New Testaments, are the goals we should desire as we grow in grace and in knowledge of Christ. Both the Law at Sinai and the sacrifice at Calvary have worked together to bring us to repentance. The Law was actually a part of God's big picture of grace, which revealed both His wrath and His mercy. "Behold therefore the goodness and severity of God: on them which fell, severity; but toward thee, goodness, if thou continue in his goodness: otherwise thou also shalt be cut off" (Romans 11:22).

Not for a moment am I directing us away from Calvary and back to what the Scripture terms the bondage of the Law. I am quick to point out that the Law did not, nor could it, save us. That took God's grace. I am merely pointing out that what the Law revealed has never changed: God alone is God, and He is in charge of His creation. This God made possible and has extended to us grace. Simply put, we owed a debt of sin, which we had no human means to pay. Christ came and, though sinless, He paid the debt of sin that we incurred. He who was without sin paid a debt which He did not owe. Ironically, the debtor goes free. That is grace.

Christ alone went to Calvary for our sins. He alone paid sin's ransom. He alone signed our pardon. Grace, amazing grace, how sweet the sound!

Chapter 3

WHAT GRACE DOESN'T DO

In some Christian circles, grace is the miracle pill: take one each morning—two on bad days—and live any way you want short of fornication and murder. How insulting to the thought of our suffering Savior at Calvary. Further, contrary to some Christian beliefs, there are specific things grace does not do. What grace doesn't do? Whoever heard of such? For a starter, that was the message the Apostle Peter delivered to Ananias and his wife, Sapphira (Acts 5). Grace could not overlook their sin. If they had allowed it, grace would have led them to repentance. Their pride prevented such. Grace stepped aside as the guillotine of judgment fell: quick and decisive.

With such an example as Ananias and Sapphira, we should consider what grace does not do. The answer is unsettling to some. Are you ready? Here goes. Grace never removed God's intense hatred for sin. Just as God is offering grace to those that will receive it, He is still the "Judge of all the earth," and in this position He is (hold onto your hats) still passing out judgment upon the earth. I want to make this point a little clearer. Not only has He judged the world in the past and will judge the world at some future time, but He is the judge of the earth—right now. Nothing escapes His awareness.

Consider again the Scripture: "Behold therefore the goodness and severity of God: on them which fell, severity; but toward thee, goodness, if thou continue in his goodness: otherwise thou also shalt be cut off" (Romans 11:22). The goodness of God refers to the moral qualities of God that we enjoy talking about and experiencing: love, mercy, longsuffering, gentleness, and kindness—to name a few. Grace certainly falls into this category of "God's goodness." Paul also draws attention to "God's severity." This refers to the moral quality of God, but it is something we don't like to talk about and would like to forget. This moral quality has to do with God's position as judge of this world—the moral caretaker of society. Dr. J. I. Packer describes this term, severity, when he writes: "The word . . . means literally "cutting off;" it denotes God's decisive withdrawal of His goodness from those who have spurned it."[1]

Paul expressed to the Romans that God's goodness to us is conditional: " . . . if thou continue in His goodness: otherwise thou also shalt be cut off" (Romans 11:22). Commentator Donald C. Stamps elaborates on this verse, making its meaning quite thought provoking. "No Christian church or ministry may presume that it will never fall under the judgment of God."[2] There was and still is a reciprocal process to God's moral attributes: we reap what we sow. Adam and Eve did. Samson did. David did, and Judas, and Ananias and his wife. If we sow faith we will follow God and reap his goodness; alternatively, if we sow disbelief we will grow apart from God and ultimately reap His severity. This is not an impulsive act of punishment, but it is the end result of the pathway of an unrepentant heart.

But some argue we're now protected by grace, so we need little focus, if any, in regards to sins we commit. Like an artist daubing colors on canvass, we paint Calvary covering our sins as we commit them. We do so without much consideration of the biblical accounts in the New Testament of those who fell under the severity of God's judgment or received warning to repent or suffer the consequences:

- Ananias and Sapphira   Acts 5:1-11
- Simon the sorcerer   Acts 8:18-24
- Herod   Acts 12:18-23
- Elymas the sorcerer   Acts 13:8-11
- Demas   Colossians 4:14
- Entire churches   Revelation 2-3

The New Testament message of grace never intended to cancel out the message of God's severity. Neither did the message intend to overlook man's sins. The message of grace offers pardon for sins through faith in the atoning blood of Jesus Christ applied to our lives by the New Birth. It offers continual pardon as we confess sins we commit. We have a twofold challenge: to experience the New Birth and to look to Christ for forgiveness of sins after our conversion. Never are we instructed by Scripture to excuse sin and to live flippantly regarding sin.

Some want grace without a conversion experience. Too many ignore the biblical doctrine that grace is applied at the New Birth. We are but to look to the conversation of Christ with Nicodemus to consider the necessity of the New Birth. Nicodemus was a good man of the Judaic faith. He knew a lot about God and the Old Testament. And I dare say he tried daily to live a righteous life. Still, Jesus challenged him to experience grace in a new and better way:

> Jesus answered and said unto him, Verily, verily, I say unto thee, Except a man be born again, he cannot see the kingdom of God. Nicodemus saith unto him, How can a man be born when he is old? can he enter the second time into his mother's womb, and be born? Jesus answered, Verily, verily, I say unto thee, Except a man be born of water and of the Spirit, he cannot enter into the kingdom of God. That which is born of the flesh is flesh; and that which is born of the Spirit is spirit. Marvel not that I said unto thee, Ye must be born again.
>
> John 3:3-7

The actions and teachings of the apostles harmonized with the New Birth message of Christ. Likewise, the New Testament letters to the believers reinforced the necessity of desiring a life conscious of living according to the morality of God, offering a balance of both judgment for sin but grace to cover one's transgression.

This then is the message which we have heard of him,

and declare unto you, that God is light, and in him is no darkness at all. If we say that we have fellowship with him, and walk in darkness, we lie, and do not the truth: But if we walk in the light, as he is in the light, we have fellowship one with another, and the blood of Jesus Christ his Son cleanseth us from all sin. If we say that we have no sin, we deceive ourselves, and the truth is not in us. If we confess our sins, he is faithful and just to forgive us our sins, and to cleanse us from all unrighteousness. If we say that we have not sinned, we make him a liar, and his word is not in us. My little children, these things write I unto you, that ye sin not. And if any man sin, we have an advocate with the Father, Jesus Christ the righteous: And he is the propitiation for our sins: and not for ours only, but also for the sins of the whole world. And hereby we do know that we know him, if we keep his commandments. He that saith, I know him, and keepeth not his commandments, is a liar, and the truth is not in him. But whoso keepeth his word, in him verily is the love of God perfected: hereby know we that we are in him. He that saith he abideth in him ought himself also so to walk, even as he walked.

I John 1:5-10; 2:1-1-6

Grace removes our sins by the substitute sacrifice at Calvary; it does not excuse us to sin freely. It is not a get-out-of-jail-free-card that removes any personal responsibility regarding how we should live. Dr. Packer expresses a balance regarding this concept:

"The Christians at Rome are not to dwell on God's goodness alone, nor on His severity alone, but to contemplate both together. Both are attributes of God—aspects, that is, of His revealed character. Both appear alongside each other in the economy of grace. Both must be acknowledged together if God is to be truly known."[3]

Where did man get the idea that God's grace canceled out the responsibility of God as judge of all the earth (Genesis 18:25)? What has caused us to drift so far with the current of leniency toward sin? Here's some thoughts that may give insight.

One, we don't realize how a Holy God views sin. Sin is as offensive to God as devastating diseases are to our society. When we consider the Prophet Isaiah's depiction of the crucified Messiah, it offers some awareness of how God views sin (Isaiah 53). The death of Christ had to be so horrible that somewhere in the process God could proclaim, "Enough! I've seen enough punishment to compensate for man's transgression." Consider how far the punishment went before God considered the debt of sin avenged. Such words as despised, rejected, grief, wounded, bruised, afflicted, smitten, oppressed, and death are used to describe the scene. Isaiah records some of the most troubling words of Scripture: "Yet it pleased the Lord to bruise him . . . . He shall see of the travail of his soul, and shall be satisfied" (Isaiah 53:10-11). Remember, all these hideous crimes were done to a sinless man, the only sinless man since Adam. How could God be pleased and satisfied to see Christ hanging on the cross and punished in this manner? There is only one plausible explanation. Sin, when compared to God's holiness, is a horrific scene, but when God viewed the scene of Calvary, it satisfied the ultimate requirement for sin to be punished. God was pleased because Christ's punishment for sin (that He never committed) was so severe that He could extend grace to all mankind and for all sins.

Two, we have allowed society to establish the norm (right and wrong) instead of the Word of God being our rulebook. We must realize, though sin may be considered "norm" by society, it still is sin in God's sight. The "norm" in Noah's day was considered "sin" in God's perception. In fact, to do right (considering our nature and the deceitfulness of sin and Satan) is often considered unnecessary by society; whereas, wrong is often viewed more acceptable by society. Modern day "political correctness" has silenced society on certain sins. Man's laws have usurped the laws of God. Many of man's laws are in blatant opposition to God's Laws. A recent example is the trend of society to change regulations regarding actions previously deemed abnormal behavior as being normal. Prior to the 1970's the American Psychiatric Association deemed homosexuality as abnormal behavior. Not only have they reversed their stand, they have advocated for laws that prosecute professional counselors who use conversion therapy to help gay teens become heterosexual. We have seen a quantum leap of society into what was previously deemed unacceptable behavior: abortion, indecent dress, legalizing drugs, co-ed dorms, unisex restrooms, unwed pregnancies, same-sex marriage, body piercing, and tattoos. We have created a new term for the unthinkable: "sexting" (young people sending nude pictures of themselves via cellphones). In a single century we moved from the Bible as a textbook to it being banned from the teachers desk. We are now subjugated to having those confused about their gender, to be favored by their choice of restrooms. To advocate previously held principles of decency is considered closed mindedness. "There is a generation that are pure in their own eyes, and yet is not washed from their filthiness" (Proverbs 30:12). I like how The Message explains this verse: "Don't imagine yourself to be quite presentable when you haven't had a bath in weeks."$_{MSG}$ A personal pet-peeve is folks attending funerals looking like they just got in from surfing. We dress-up for the Derby; we dress down for the death of a friend. Dignity died, and society had it cremated.

Three, we don't recognize our own sinfulness, as God sees sin, often justifying our sins rather than seeking forgiveness. "The heart is deceitful above all things, and desperately wicked: who can know it?" (Jeremiah 17:9). The Scripture warns of a society desiring sin so very much that God sends delusion, and they no longer view sin as sinful; rather, they view sin as conditional. "And with all deceivableness of unrighteousness in them that perish; because they received not the love of the truth, that they might be saved. And for this cause God shall send them strong delusion, that they should believe a lie: That they all might be damned who believed not the truth, but had pleasure in unrighteousness" (II Thessalonians 2:10-13). It seems strange that a person who once lived for God could not perceive a delusive lie? But in this case of willingly overriding what one knows is right and choosing to do wrong, both revelation of truth and delusion comes from the same source: God. Delusion sent from God is justified when an individual receives truth from God but constantly desires a sinful lifestyle. Continual justification of sin leads to a seared conscience. The remedy for sin is not personal justification;

rather, it is justification from God that comes through genuine repentance and reliance upon grace extended by Calvary's sacrifice.

Fourth, we have created what Dr. Packer calls a "Santa Claus theology," that God is basically only good—and thus could not punish people, or else He would cease to be good. Since we see Him as good (void of any inclination to punish mankind for sin), He cannot be bad (to punish mankind for sin would be bad, so he can't punish mankind). We now have control over God, holding over His head the "good God" theme. The error here comes because of our perception, or lack thereof, of sin as being bad. Since we've reached a point in our thought process that sin no longer disturbs God, we no longer need a savior, and whether I'm good or bad doesn't matter, for God's goodness will be extended to all, regardless. This twentieth century "good God liberalism" reduces Christ's atoning cross to mere needless suffering. How apostate!

This takes us a step farther into the question of "Why do bad things happen to good people?" The error of our "good God theology" generally comes to light in some disappointment or by some disaster, and this error leads us to this false conclusion: since our "good God" didn't come to our rescue, life is out of God's control—God can't do anything about it. Additional apostasy! Dr. Packer concludes regarding this "good God" false theology: " . . . a God who is all goodness and no severity tends to confirm men in a fatalistic and pessimistic attitude to life."[4]

Many view God as good in the New Testament (due to His grace) and bad in the Old Testament (due to His severity). God's goodness is not confined to the pages of the New Testament, while God's severity is not confined to the Old Testament. Each is present in both the testaments. Consider the Old Testament general history of God's people, Israel. God delivered them from Egyptian bondage (goodness) while He punished Egypt (severity). He later punished Northern Israel by giving them over to Assyrian captivity (severity) although He had spared the Assyrian capital, Nineveh, during the preaching of Jonah the prophet (goodness). Later, the Babylonians captured the Assyrians (severity), yet Judah (the southern part of Israel) is spared the assault of the Babylonians (goodness). The Babylonians later conquered Judah, taking them into seventy years of captivity (severity), but God delivered them after seventy years (goodness). This is not a "good cop, bad cop" scenario of God, manipulating man into serving Him out of obligation or fear; rather, it is the principles under which God governs the universe. The bad will eventually be punished; the good will eventually be rewarded. These are eternal principles!

In studying the above-mentioned events, there was a common denominator—obedience brought God's goodness; disobedience brought God's severity. These events were not coincidental occurrences: they were portrayals of divine retribution—good for good, severity for evil. At all time God is in charge. Babylon didn't conquer simply because it had the military capabilities; they did so as a matter of carrying out the will of God (severity). Neither did Cyrus and Artaxerxes, kings of Persia, simply decide to let Ezra and Nehemiah return from captivity back to their homeland; they did so because God ordained it and placed it in their hearts to do so (goodness).

Some challenge who gave God the right to inflict severity upon others. Isn't this cruel of God? Doesn't this make Him unholy? Again, I borrow from Dr. Packer's biblical explanations. "God's wrath is always judicial—that is, it is the wrath of the judge, administering justice."[5] God is obligated as judge of the universe to make decisions, and these decisions are always just. We may not completely understand why He chose to act as He did, but neither do we know all the details. God is all-knowing, and His decisions are always right.

Consider the biblical example of the Book of Esther. The king is Ahasuerus. Mordecai is a righteous Jew who saved the king's life from an assignation plot. Wicked Haman is the villain (jealous of Mordecai) who bends the king's ear to punish Mordecai and his people. The Jewish people become the victims. You must read the book to get all the details of the story. As the story unfolds, wicked and deceitful Haman built a gallows one hundred and fifty feet tall (an unsubtle hint of his prideful heart), upon which he plotted to hang Mordecai. Not only this, but he plotted to slaughter the entire Jewish race. In a divine drama of events, King Ahasuerus found out about this devious plot. He ordered wicked Haman to be hung on the gallows Haman had built to hang righteous Mordecai. The king elevated Mordecai next to himself.

That's the story; here's the point. I make it in the form of a question. Did King Ahasuerus have the right to pass such sentence? The answer of course is yes, for his position as king entitled such action. The same is true today, for a judge, according to the laws of the land, has the right to pass sentence—though it may seem severe. Not only does the judge have the right, he is also under obligation. He is sworn to uphold the laws of his or her jurisdiction. Such is the case with God's wrath. It is always judicial—that is, it is the wrath of the Judge of the universe, administering justice. Who made Him the judge? It came about because of His position as creator. He is bound to keep order in the creation He spoke into existence. As God administers justice, wrongdoers are punished, according to the laws of God. It is no wonder atheists decry the biblical message of creation. If Genesis is correct, we are bound as the creation to serve the Creator. The Creator is bound to rule His creation. Even an avowed atheist would acknowledge a judge is bound to perform his duty.

Dr. Packer offers a second rational for the severity of God. "God's wrath in the Bible is something people choose for themselves. Before hell is an experience inflicted by God, it is a state for which a person himself opts by retreating from the light which God shines in his heart to lead him to Himself."[6]

But, we ask, "What about those who have never read the Bible or heard the Bible taught?" Paul answers this question. By nature—without the Bible—man has a basic knowledge of right and wrong. God endowed him with enough knowledge to choose to at least seek after his creator. And if we seek Him we shall find Him, for He has been in pursuit of us ever since the fall from the garden. Idolatry and atheism is a decision that tramples over the footprints of God: the idolater follows after his foolish imagination and creates a deity; the atheist turns his vision inward and becomes his own deity.

> "For the wrath of God is revealed from heaven against all ungodliness and unrighteousness of men, who hold the truth in unrighteousness; Because that which may be known of God is manifest in them; for God hath shewed it unto them. For the invisible things of him from the creation of the world are clearly seen, being understood by the things that are made, even his eternal power and Godhead; so that they are without excuse: Because that, when they knew God, they glorified him not as God, neither were thankful; but became vain in their imaginations, and their foolish heart was darkened. Professing themselves

to be wise, they became fools, And changed the glory
of the uncorruptible God into an image made like to
corruptible man, and to birds, and fourfooted beasts,
and creeping things.

Romans 1:18-23

God has written "universal laws of nature" upon every conscience. Every society knows murder and rape and theft are wrong.
Why? These are universal laws of nature written upon the human
heart. Those who break these laws are removed from society. Any
society who has no such laws is called uncivilized. A society must
completely abandon the conscience to live apart from the universal
laws of nature. This, of course, would be a choice.

A person who breaks the universal laws of nature is called a
sinner and is without excuse. To choose sin is to choose the result of
sin itself. The end result is a coming judgment (not without biblical
warning), which many have challenged is a myth, but to challenge
the Judge of the universe will not prevent Him from performing
His judicial duties. Dr. Packer concludes, "Nobody stands under the
wrath of God except those who have chosen to do so."[7]

Likewise, as God's severity is manifest because of mankind's
choice to abandon scriptural principles, God's goodness is reserved
for those who seek Him. For this reason we should study and revere
God's Word, and we should cling to the righteousness described in
the Holy Scripture.

Even grace cannot overlook sin; grace can only postpone judgment as God draws us to repentance. Grace works in our lives as we
seek after God and the sacrifice of Calvary to cleanse us from all
unrighteousness. Grace leads us through the maze of snares, adversity, and deception we encounter on our journey to heaven. "But he
giveth more grace. Wherefore he saith, God resisteth the proud, but
giveth grace unto the humble" (James 4:6). The fountain of grace
never dries up for those who desire it with a sincere heart.

Chapter 4

HOW GRACE IS APPLIED

With the emphasis we place on grace, one might get the idea grace is the Savior; hence, we should exalt grace, idolize grace, worship grace. To the contrary, grace is not who saved us. Grace is the means by which God made possible our salvation. Christ's sacrificial sacrifice at Calvary unleashed a reservoir of grace. Prior to Calvary, the unfolding plan of God allowed Him to postpone our judgment, while He accomplished the means whereby our sins could be forever remitted.

Let's use an example to better explain grace. We could say that a certain populace was saved by an airlift. Note, the terminology states that the airlift saved them, but this is not really the case. The airlift was simply the means by which the food, water, and medical supplies came to the impoverished people. Without the airlift, all the supplies in the world would be useless to this people. Further, unless the people accepted the airlifted provisions—eating, drinking, and applying the medical supplies to their physical needs—they would not be saved. The savior in this case, the one responsible for their salvation, are the ones who prepared and carried out the airlift. Such is the means of our eternal salvation. We could describe grace—God's unmerited favor toward us—as the vehicle that delivered salvation to mankind. Consider the writings of Paul:

> For the grace of God that bringeth salvation hath appeared to all men, Teaching us that, denying ungodliness and worldly lusts, we should live soberly, righteously, and godly, in this present world; Looking for that blessed hope, and the glorious appearing of the great God and our Saviour Jesus Christ; Who gave himself for us, that he might redeem us from all iniquity, and purify unto himself a peculiar people, zealous of good works.

Titus 2:11-14

The Lord Jesus Christ is the Savior. Grace is the vehicle, or the strategy of God, that brought salvation instead of wrath. Salvation became possible by the death, burial, and resurrection of the Lord; however, this means of salvation only works when applied to an individual. How then does Christ's death become applicable to an individual? It is applied through personal faith and the experience of the New Birth. A familiar scriptural example affirms this. Nicodemus, a religious leader of Judaism, came to Jesus by night—evidently affirming that he believed Christ was the Messiah but fearing for his position in Judaism. In the narrative, he didn't necessarily ask how to be saved, but Jesus perceived his seeking heart and answered the unspoken question of how can a man be sure regarding his salvation. Jesus explained, "Verily, verily, I say unto thee, Except a man be born of water and of the Spirit, he cannot enter into the kingdom of God" (John 3:5). From the Scripture we realize the New Birth requires two components: faith and obedience. Faith is an attitude of trust that allows us to open our hearts to the invisible God of Scripture. Obedience is an act of submission to God's commands in Scripture. These commands include repentance, water baptism, and Spirit baptism. Repentance is an acknowledgement of personal sin, a sense of God's displeasure, and a sincere desire to turn from sin and unto God. Water baptism into Christ Jesus applies Christ's atoning death—the payment for sins—to our lives. The Holy Spirit baptism is Christ's personal entrance into the life of the believer.

The New Birth does not merely cause God to postpone judgment for sin, as was the case in the Old Testament, when animal sacrifices were the demanded means of salvation for Israel. During the Old Testament era, even God's judgment for idolatry among Israel and various peoples of the earth was postponed—in some cases for centuries—as God waited for them to repent, but more so as He waited for the appearance of the Savior into the world. The Gentile community, alienated from the true God, escaped destruction as God stalled judgment in anticipation of His redemptive plan at Calvary. The terminology "God winked at" refers to His confidence in the power of the crucified Christ to change lives in the future. "Forasmuch then as we are the offspring of God, we ought not to think that the Godhead is like unto gold, or silver, or stone, graven by art and man's device. And the times of this ignorance God winked at; but now commandeth all men every where to repent" (Acts 17:29-30).

During the time of the Mosaic Law, since animal sacrifice was insufficient to remove sin, God annually pushed forward the judgment for Israel's sins, patiently awaiting the ultimate sacrifice: Christ's atoning death. Each year the annual sacrificial atonements were made, and each year God rendered the same judgment: postponed, to be reconsidered next year, conviction delayed. This judgment was stamped annually upon the charges brought against Israel. After Calvary the charges of mankind's sins were not stamped with a "judgment postponed" verdict; conversely, they were stamped "pardoned." If someone searched for the indictments, they found the persons transgressions completely erased, blotted out by the blood of Christ's sacrifice. The Scripture explains that Christ became the propitiation for our sin before God. Simply stated, the death of Christ was accepted as payment for our debt of sin. Our debt of sin wasn't just overlooked, Christ's sacrificial offering paid the debt in full; God never again brought up the charges, for they no longer existed. This placed sin in a new light: since there is a means of redemption, mankind became responsible for delivering his sins to the redeemer. God no longer winks at the idolatry of the gentiles; rather, God demands repentance of such. Christ challenged Nicodemus, representing the people with whom God had been in a covenant relationship for fifteen hundred years: they had to be born again, for the Old Covenant did not remove their sins, it merely postponed judgment. This extremely religious man's expression exposed his challenge of Christ's command for the New Birth, but Jesus pleaded: "Marvel not that I said unto thee, Ye must be born again" (John 3:7).

By Adam's disobedience in the garden, all humankind inherited a moral corruption that motivates them to do evil. This is not to say that we are guilty by reason of Adam's sin; rather, we are guilty because we live according to the nature we inherited from Adam, which is a nature that leads us to eventually commit sin. Therefore, "All have sinned," Paul wrote. However, Paul did not suggest we are hopelessly enslaved to sin, but he directs us to find forgiveness and to live an overcoming life through Christ.

> Let not sin therefore reign in your mortal body, that ye should obey it in the lusts thereof. Neither yield ye your members as instruments of unrighteousness unto sin: but yield yourselves unto God, as those that are alive from the dead, and your members as instruments of righteousness unto God. For sin shall not have dominion over you: for ye are not under the law, but under grace. What then? shall we sin, because we are not under the law, but under grace? God forbid. Know ye not, that to whom ye yield yourselves servants to obey, his servants ye are to whom ye obey; whether of sin unto death, or of obedience unto righteousness.
>
> Romans 5:17-21

Jesus Christ committed no sin, nor did He inherit the tendency toward moral corruption, for He was conceived of the Spirit of God rather than the seed of Adam. Still, He submitted to the wages of sin: death. And He suffered severely—as if He had sinned—in order to appease the judgment for sin. By the obedience of the Lord Jesus unto death, humankind can now experience reclaimed fellowship and favor with God, having their sins remitted, and they can be inclined toward the morality of God. This is made possible through our faith in Christ's provision at Calvary and our obedience to Christ regarding the New Birth experience.

> For if by one man's offence death reigned by one; much more they which receive abundance of grace and of the gift of righteousness shall reign in life by one, Jesus Christ. Therefore as by the offence of one judgment came upon all men to condemnation; even so by the righteousness of one the free gift came upon all men unto justification of life. For as by one man's disobedience many were made sinners, so by the obedience of one shall many be made righteous. Moreover the law entered, that the offence might abound. But where sin abounded, grace did much more abound: That as sin hath reigned unto death, even so might grace reign through righteousness unto eternal life by Jesus Christ our Lord.
>
> Romans 5:17-21

Adam and Eve did not die physically the day they disobeyed God (for they lived many years after their sin and expulsion from the garden), but their physical bodies did start the aging (death) process, and they experienced an instantaneous spiritual death. They lost their God-created innocence, sin dominated their thought process, and their constant communion with God ended: they died. That is why, to reverse the curse, we must be born again. The New Birth experience restores our relationship with God. In our spiritual re-birth Christ's death is applied to our sins. We are restored to Eden innocence (as if we had never sinned) and fellowship with God, and the natural inclination to sin is resisted and ultimately constrained by the power of the indwelling Holy Spirit. None of Christ's acts at Calvary were symbolic: Christ literally experienced the unbelievable pain and humiliation of the Roman crucifixion, was buried, and after three days resurrected with a transformed body. These literal acts that purchased the means of our salvation are personally applied to us spiritually as:

- We acknowledge our faith in Him (recognizing His ultimate sacrifice for our sins),
- We confess and repent of our sins (a typology of His death),
- We are baptized (a typology of His burial, for at baptism in the name of the Lord Jesus Christ we identify with Him as Savior, His death is applied to our sins, thus His death pays our penalty of sin, and we will not be condemned to death for our sins), and finally,
- We experience the Holy Spirit baptism (a typology of His resurrection). We now have the power that raised Christ from the dead resident within us.

Paul explains the process of the New Birth and how the death of the sinless Christ is ample coverage for our debt of sin; further, the New Birth empowers us to overcome the sins of the fallen nature:

> Know ye not, that so many of us as were baptized into Jesus Christ were baptized into his death? Therefore we are buried with him by baptism into death: that like as Christ was raised up from the dead by the glory of the Father, even so we also should walk in newness of life. For if we have been planted together in the likeness of his death, we shall be also in the likeness of his resurrection: Knowing this, that our old man is crucified with him, that the body of sin might be destroyed, that henceforth we should not serve sin. For he that is dead is freed from sin. Now if we be dead with Christ, we believe that we shall also live with him: Knowing that Christ being raised from the dead dieth no more; death hath no more dominion over him. For in that he died, he died unto sin once but in that he liveth, he liveth unto God.
>
> Romans 6:3-10

Some suggest the acts of water baptism and Holy Spirit baptism are insignificant (merely visible expressions because one has already experienced the New Birth by faith), and that we don't need to partake of such; rather, we are to simply believe on the Lord Jesus Christ (sometimes referred to as the sinners prayer) and openly express our faith. This is partially true, for faith is a prerequisite for salvation, but the Bible is a book of specifics, and biblical directives regarding the New Birth include water and Spirit baptism as essentials for the New Birth. In short, many have experienced Christ in various ways but have not yet experienced the New Birth. This statement is not to diminish one's personal experience with Christ, but it is to challenge the concept that salvation is available through multiple and non-specific means. We'll share specifics regarding the New Birth shortly, but first, recognize the importance of specifics in Scripture. Consider Christ's prayer in the garden: "If it be possible, let this cup pass from me." The humanity of Jesus Christ agonized in prayer just moments before his arrest and a few hours before His crucifixion, desiring that man's redemption come about without His crucifixion. Consider this loose paraphrase: "Since Calvary will be unbelievably painful and humiliating, and since I've never personally sinned, let's just dispense with the literal crucifixion and create a symbolic means of salvation. Let's merely proclaim that the Savior has come as the symbolic Lamb of God, and therefore all that want to be saved are saved by simply expressing their allegiance to Him." No, this is not the way it happened. Jesus literally experienced the arrest, trial, beating, and ultimately the crucifixion. Likewise, when we believe in His atoning death and want it applied to our lives, we should literally experience the New Birth of repentance, water baptism in His saving name, and receiving the Holy Spirit. Without exception, the first church converts did not challenge the need for repentance, water baptism in the name of the Lord Jesus Christ, and the infilling of the Holy Spirit. The apostles commanded such, and the believers embraced their teaching. Why should we challenge these biblical precedents?

There are three classifications of people within the New Testament: Israelites, also referred to as Jews (a title popularized after the Babylonian captivity that referred to all descendants of Abraham); Samaritans (referring to descendants of the ten northern tribes of Israel who had intermarried with a non-Jewish populace, drifted away from the Mosaic Law, built their own temple—rejecting the temple in Jerusalem—with their own priesthood, had their own lineage of kings, and considered Samaria their capitol instead of Jerusalem); and Gentiles (of no Jewish ancestry). Consider the following examples of conversion of each of these groups:

Israelites

The initial believers in the upper room were Israelites who followed after Christ, therefore we can assume they were already baptized into Christ as His disciples. Their experience of Spirit baptism, evidenced by speaking in an unknown (unlearned) tongue (language) established a common denominator that is present in other Spirit baptism examples:

> And when the day of Pentecost was fully come, they were all with one accord in one place. And suddenly there came a sound from heaven as of a rushing mighty wind, and it filled all the house where they were sitting. And there appeared unto them cloven tongues like as of fire, and it sat upon each of them. And they were all filled with the Holy Ghost, and began to speak with other tongues, as the Spirit gave them utterance.
>
> Acts 2:1-4

A multitude of Israelites from around the world had journeyed to Jerusalem for the Feast of Pentecost. If a map is drawn of the countries represented that day, it will show that nations from all directions of the world were present in Jerusalem. When the Spirit entered the believers, they spoke in languages that were native of these countries represented. This phenomenon caught the attention of the crowd, and some sought out what was happening. The phenomena of tongues, along with the preaching of the Apostle Peter, convinced many that Jesus was the Christ. They then requested how they might be saved.

Now when they heard this, they were pricked in their

heart, and said unto Peter and to the rest of the apostles, Men and brethren, what shall we do? Then Peter said unto them, Repent, and be baptized every one of you in the name of Jesus Christ for the remission of sins, and ye shall receive the gift of the Holy Ghost. For the promise is unto you, and to your children, and to all that are afar off, even as many as the Lord our God shall call. And with many other words did he testify and exhort, saying, Save yourselves from this untoward generation.   Then they that gladly received his word were baptized: and the same day there were added unto them about three thousand souls. And they continued stedfastly in the apostles' doctrine and fellowship, and in breaking of bread, and in prayers.

Acts 2:37-42

Samaritans

Therefore they that were scattered abroad went every where preaching the word. Then Philip went down to the city of Samaria, and preached Christ unto them.   And the people with one accord gave heed unto those things which Philip spake, hearing and seeing the miracles which he did. For unclean spirits, crying with loud voice, came out of many that were possessed with them: and many taken with palsies, and that were lame, were healed. And there was great joy in that city.

Acts 8:4-8

But when they believed Philip preaching... the name of Jesus Christ, they were baptized, both men and women.

Acts 8:12

> Now when the apostles which were at Jerusalem heard that Samaria had received the word of God, they sent unto them Peter and John: Who, when they were come down, prayed for them, that they might receive the Holy Ghost: (For as yet he was fallen upon none of them: only they were baptized in the name of the Lord Jesus.) Then laid they their hands on them, and they received the Holy Ghost.

> Acts 8:14-17

It is significant to note that the Scripture doesn't state the Samaritans spoke in tongues, but we can certainly assume this to be the case, for Simon the sorcerer offered money to purchase the ability to lay his hands upon seekers that they would receive the Holy Spirit baptism. Something so phenomenal happened that Simon desired to be in on the supernatural—of the observable results of Holy Spirit baptism only speaking in tongues would have elicited such a request. "And when Simon saw that through laying on of the apostles' hands the Holy Ghost was given, he offered them money, Saying, Give me also this power, that on whomsoever I lay hands, he may receive the Holy Ghost" (Acts 8:18-19).

Gentiles

> While Peter yet spake these words, the Holy Ghost fell on all them which heard the word. And they of the circumcision which believed were astonished, as many as came with Peter, because that on the Gentiles also was poured out the gift of the Holy Ghost. For they heard them speak with tongues, and magnify God. Then answered Peter, Can any man forbid water, that these should not be baptized, which have received the Holy Ghost as well as we? And he commanded them to be baptized in the name of the Lord. Then prayed they him to tarry certain days.

> Acts 10:44-48

These three groups represent all people of the Apostles' day: Israelite, Samaritan, and Gentile. There is a simple thread of consistency in the conversions of all. All were seekers of God; therefore, we can assume they manifested a repented life. Secondly, all were baptized in water in the name of Jesus as Lord and Savior. Contrary to the post-apostolic traditional mode of Christian baptism (This was baptism in the triune formula of father, son, and Holy Ghost, which are not names; rather, they are titles.), all early church believers were baptized specifically in the name of the Savior—Jesus Christ. This is true from both a scriptural reference and also from historical references. Thirdly, all believers experienced the Holy Spirit baptism. The uniform evidence of Holy Spirit infilling was speaking in an unlearned tongue (language) under the influence of the Holy Spirit.

There is another example that is noteworthy because it also portrays this uniform manner of Christian conversion. These converts were probably Israelites who had become disciples of John the Baptist. We're not told why, but when Paul meets them they are living in Ephesus. Though dispersed from Israel, they maintained the principles taught by John, not fully aware of the ministry of Christ nor that John had directed his disciples to follow Christ.

Disciples of John the Baptist

> And it came to pass, that, while Apollos was at Corinth, Paul having passed through the upper coasts came to Ephesus: and finding certain disciples, He said unto them, Have ye received the Holy Ghost since ye believed? And they said unto him, We have not so much as heard whether there be any Holy Ghost. And he said unto them, Unto what then were ye baptized? And they said, Unto John's baptism. Then said Paul, John verily baptized with the baptism of repentance, saying unto the people, that they should believe on him which should come after him, that is, on Christ Jesus. When they heard this, they were baptized in the name of the Lord Jesus. And when Paul had laid his hands upon them, the Holy Ghost came on them; and they spake with tongues,

49

and prophesied.

Acts 19:1-6

Once again we see the thread of consistency: water baptism in Christ's saving name and the infilling of the Holy Spirit, evidenced by speaking in tongues. These are the primary examples of New Testament Christian conversion. In each there is much more than the recitation of a sinner's prayer. Each responds in a uniform and with a noticeable manner to the extension of God's amazing grace. No one is passive in the salvation experience; rather, each one is an active participant in the salvation experience through obedience regarding water and Spirit baptism.

The vehicle of salvation is grace. Faith is the receiving hand of the individual toward this unmerited favor of God. The outstretched hand of faith is not mere acknowledgment of God, but faith incorporates obedience to His commands regarding the New birth. I certainly don't want to minimize the role faith plays in conversion, so we'll discuss faith more completely later in the book. For now let's consider that by faith we acknowledge the God of Scripture, recognize sin has separated us from His favor, and therefore we repent of our sins (true repentance is a turning away from sin and toward the Holy God) as a first step in the salvation process. Through baptism we apply to our sins Christ's atoning sacrifice at Calvary. We acknowledge that He died in our place and for our sins. We recognize and identify with His death for our sins through baptism in His name. Peter proclaimed: "Neither is there salvation in any other: for there is none other name under heaven given among men, whereby we must be saved" (Acts 4:12). Paul further proclaimed, "And whatsoever ye do in word or deed, do all in the name of the Lord Jesus, giving thanks to God and the Father by him" (Colossians 3:17). After we identify with Christ's death through baptism, He affirms our status by filling us with Himself: this is the Holy Spirit experience, which is evidenced by speaking in an unlearned tongue through the anointing of the omnipotent and omniscient God.

Of course I am aware that some wonderful people of the Christian community challenge this teaching as being confrontational, others reject it as unnecessary and narrow minded, and some perceive it as fanaticism, even heretical. However, no matter our church affiliation, we cannot honestly deny the fact that water baptism in the name of the Savior, and the infilling of the Holy Spirit—evidenced by tongues speaking—is obvious in Scripture. I would encourage anyone reading this who has not experienced such to sincerely search out the Scriptures regarding water baptism and humbly seek the experience of the Holy Spirit baptism. The Lord will not deny a sincere seeker of the Holy Spirit baptism. Jesus expressed: "If ye then, being evil, know how to give good gifts unto your children: how much more shall your heavenly Father give the Holy Spirit to them that ask him?" (Luke 11:13). As a true believer one does not want to reject an experience in God that is not only biblical, but the New Birth is necessary in order to walk in the Spirit. It is the indwelling Spirit that does the continued work of grace and makes believers ready for the ultimate and final work of grace: the transformation and rapture of believers.

Chapter 5

WHATEVER HAPPENED TO THE LAW

The Old Testament Law, referred to as the Mosaic Law and Torah, consists of four categories: the moral law, the civil law, the dietary regulations, and the ceremonial (sacrificial system) law. Each of these categories held specific significance: each reflected the command for Israel's separation unto the Lord and separation from evil. Let's consider each.

The moral law taught Israel the rules required by God for holy living: they were associated with God's character. They defined God. These stipulated the requirements for Israel to fulfill the demand of God in Scripture "to be holy." These laws had God's interest as their focus.

The civil law taught Israel the legal, social, and sanitary rules under which they were to operate as a nation. These laws focused on how to treat each other. They had the goodwill of mankind as their focus.

The dietary regulations focused on health issues. It contrasted with the diet acquired during the four hundred years in Egypt. These laws were specifically designed to prevent premature death, and they served to show a separation of Israel from the gentile nations around them. These laws had the individual as their focus. The ceremonial law outlined stipulations for Israel's worship of the one true God, gave instruction for the offering of multiple sacrifices, and demanded the observance of certain feast days. Scattered throughout these categories were regulations for cleansing (both spiritual and physical). These all included the concept of Israel being separated unto the Lord and from the other idolatrous nations of the earth. God entered into a covenant relationship with Israel unlike any other relationship with other nations or individuals. The covenant relationship demanded certain commitments from Israel, and it offered certain benefits for compliance. These laws had separation from the worldly system and separation unto the one true God as their focus.

The Law was not a document enslaving Israel to the bondage of a deity; it was a proclamation of their liberation of four hundred years of human bondage. Much of Torah reflected the lifestyles of those righteous people who lived before the Law: Enoch, Noah, Abraham, and others. The giving of the Law to Moses was the first time instruction for righteous living was in written form. After the giving of the Law, all Israelites knew God's expectations, because the expectations were written. The Ten Commandments were etched in stone, and Moses wrote the laws as God revealed them to him on Mt. Sinai. The priests consistently read and interpreted the law to the people. Because of the written law, it became obvious when one broke one of the commands. The ceremonial law included specific sacrifices demanded for specific sins. Further, in breaking a law, one recognized he had sinned against God—not necessarily because he sensed guilt, but because the written Law said so. The dictates of Torah classified him a sinner who needed forgiveness for having broken the Law. At this point he needed direction as to how he could have such sins rescinded. No problem. God incorporated into the Mosaic Law a ceremonial system of sacrifice for the atonement of sins, but man had to obey the plan.

Israel had a choice in accepting or rejecting the covenant God offered them. Like the covenant of marriage, Torah was a covenant relationship between Israel (as a nation but also as individuals) and God. As God's representative, Moses read the Law to Israel and gave them the chance to accept or reject the covenant. Israel said yes, thus began a nation committed to following God's dictates. By this unique covenant, Israel promised to serve only Jehovah—idolatry would be punished—out of love and appreciation for Him as their creator, sustainer, and provider; furthermore, they were to forever acknowledge Him as their deliverer from Egyptian bondage and Lord over their lives. They thoroughly understood what it was like to be under a cruel and oppressive master, and in contrast, they chose to serve a God who truly cared about them. This was a privilege, for God specifically selected them out of an idolatrous world. While other nations worshipped multiple gods, Israel was to keep alive the message, "Hear, O Israel: The Lord our God is one Lord: And thou shalt love the Lord thy God with all thine heart, and with all thy soul, and with all thy might" (Deuteronomy 6:4-5).

Key in the covenant between God and Israel was a specifically designed plan and place for worship. The religious ceremonies were done within a fenced enclosure that housed a courtyard (an altar for sacrifices sat strategically at the entrance to the courtyard) and a tent that served as the primary place of worship. Referred to as The Tabernacle in the wilderness, Israel literally encamped around this place of worship. The Tabernacle ceremonies were the center of their daily lives. Later, the temple in Jerusalem replaced this portable sanctuary.

Inside the sacred tent were three pieces of specifically designed furnishings used daily in a ritualistic form of worship: a candelabra to give light (representing illumination of truth), a table on which fresh bread was placed (representing consumption of God's Word), and an altar on which the priests burned incense (representing prayer and worship). Beyond a divider within the tent sat a furnishing called the Ark of the Covenant (often referred to as the Ark of God or simply the Ark). This important piece of furniture was a rather small rectangular shaped wooden chest (approximately four feet long, two and a half feet wide, and two and a half feet high) overlaid with gold. God referred to the top covering of the Ark as the Mercy Seat, or the abode of His mercy. On each end of the Mercy Seat, two angels (carved from a piece of gold) spread their wings forward over the seat. They represented God's continued protection. Moses placed inside the Ark a copy of the Ten Commandments (representing all of God's Law), a pot of manna (representing God's miraculous provision during the forty years of wilderness wondering), and Aaron's rod that budded (representing God's divine authority over Israel).

The divided portion of the tent housing the Ark represented the throne room of God; therefore, it represented God's abode, His favor, and His mercy, but it also represented His judgment. Once a year the high priest went into this forbidden room behind the divider and into God's presence, where he sprinkled blood from a slain animal onto the mercy seat—representing death to Israel because of their sins and mercy because of the appeasing sacrifice. As long as Israel acknowledged their covenant relationship with God—by serving Him as the one and only true God—His presence, referred to as *Shekinah* (a Hebrew word meaning dwelling), appeared as a visible manifestation of God in this throne room. During a time when Israel was out of God's favor, God allowed the Ark to be taken by the enemy (I Samuel 4:11), as if God had departed from their midst. Later, during the reign of David, the Ark was retrieved and brought to Jerusalem, where it remained, first in a tent, then in the temple built by King Solomon. As far as we know, the Ark remained in Jerusalem until the destruction of Solomon's Temple. We are uncertain as to the history of the Ark from that time forward. Today, Israel is without the Ark; however, in the prophecy of Revelation, during the hardest trial of Israel's existence, the Ark reappears: "And the temple of God was opened in heaven, and there was seen in his temple the ark of his testament: and there were lightnings, and voices, and thunderings, and an earthquake, and great hail" (Revelation 11:19). During this darkest hour of Israel's existence, the appearance of the Ark will offer hope that God is with them.

Unfortunately, the people of Israel reached a point in which they lived as if the Ark's presence unconditionally guaranteed God's favor, mercy, and protection. They erred in assuming a symbol of God's presence assured them of God's favor—even though they didn't maintain their covenant relationship. This covenant relationship included both a love relationship and a faith relationship, both which many abandoned. Furthermore, they did not fully comprehend that the sacrificial animals were insufficient to obtain God's favor, for only God's grace—His very nature—allowed the sacrifices to appease His imminent judgment. Over time, Israel trampled God's grace by their repeated sins (specifically idolatry), and they not only lost their favored position with God, they also incurred His judgment. Further, when they broke the covenant, they lost God's protection. On more than one occasion, God allowed nations who were less righteous than Israel to bring judgment upon them. This resulted in the Assyrian captivity of the ten northern tribes in the eighth century BC (the southern tribes were spared this destruction due to their continued covenant with God), the Babylonian exile in the sixth century BC (which lasted seventy years), the destruction of Israel as a nation in the second century AD, and finally the Diaspora that lasted for almost two millenniums.

Since the covenant was conditional, the animal sacrifices did not suffice for Israel's continual breaking of the covenant. Sin carried the seed of multiple consequences, one of these being Divine judgment. The debt of sin must be paid: a Divinely established universal principle. The Mosaic sacrificial system was a temporary fix for mankind's sin; it stayed God's judgment while God looked forward to the redemptive plan He envisioned at the creation. God initiated a prototype of Calvary in the Garden of Eden when he killed an animal and made literal coverings for Adam and Eve. The skins from the dead animal did much more than cover their nakedness, the death of the animal symbolically covered their sin. This substitute sacrifice in the garden was a preview of a perfect plan yet to come: Christ and Calvary.

> For the law having a shadow of good things to come, and not the very image of the things, can never with those sacrifices which they offered year by year continually make the comers thereunto perfect. For then would they not have ceased to be offered? because that the worshippers once purged should have had no more conscience of sins. But in those sacrifices there is a remembrance again made of sins every year. For it is not possible that the blood of bulls and of goats should take away sins.
>
> Hebrews 10:1-4

When Jesus came into the world, Israel's hope remained in the operation of the Law; consequently, they crucified the Lamb of God. In rejecting Christ, they continued to trust in something that was temporary, but the ceremonial law was a mere symbol of the salvation planned through Christ. Moreover, the Jewish religious leaders rejected the Incarnation (God embodied in Christ), and the sincere Israelite still clung to the Old Covenant for redemption. They focused their faith on animal sacrifices—the ceremonial law, which could not save them—and rejected the perfect sacrifice: Jesus Christ. For the nation of Israel, Christ became an obstacle between them and the God with whom they had entered a covenant relationship. They rejected the one and only Lamb of God—the only sacrifice capable of eradicating sin—therefore Israel remained in her sin.

> But Israel, which followed after the law of righteousness, hath not attained to the law of righteousness. Wherefore? Because they sought it not by faith, but as it were by the works of the law. For they stumbled at that stumblingstone; As it is written, Behold, I lay in Zion a stumblingstone and rock of offence: and whosoever believeth on him shall not be ashamed.

> Romans 9:31-33

Christ offered to Israel a new hope: a complete covenant. This New Covenant did not abolish the Old Testament Law; rather, it adapted the principles of the Law into the New Covenant. The Old Covenant became complete in that it now had an acceptable sacrifice. Rather than being totally discarded, the Old Covenant received completeness in Christ.

Consider the Old Covenant incompleteness. The blood of animals could not remit sin, nor did it possess the ability to change mankind's sinful nature; consequently, man's guilt remained, and he continued to default to his sinful nature. After Calvary the old sacrificial system that was incapable of remitting man's sins was made complete by the perfect lamb sacrificed on Calvary. Christ explained, "Think not that I am come to destroy the law, or the prophets: I am not come to destroy, but to fulfill" (Matthew 5:17).

God never intended for His people to disregard His rules of righteous living included in the moral laws; instead, Jesus taught our righteousness must exceed the righteousness of the Scribes and

Pharisees. What did He mean by this statement? Were we to add additional rules? I say no. Adding more rules would amplify the existing problem. The Israelites majored on the external, the visible, the attention getting works of the Law, failing to realize these acts were insufficient to save them. Jesus called for attention to be given, not only to the outer man, but also to the heart of man. Christ challenged humanity to focus on heart issues, from which all external sins are committed.

Christianity didn't abandon Judaism; rather, it completed its imperfections. Christianity doesn't necessarily introduce grace, it continues the work of grace first shown to Adam and Eve after their transgression. Christianity doesn't lower spiritual expectations; it elevates relationship with God to a higher level. Christianity doesn't wait for the believer to fall into sin, it draws a line in our lives before we fail, and the indwelling Holy Spirit empowers us with overcoming grace. Still, like the Law, Christianity demands that salvation is only possible through a sacrificial lamb, but unlike the Law, Christianity insists that salvation was made possible by Christ's death: God's chosen Lamb. Further, salvation cannot be earned by the works of the Law; it is the gift of God made possible by His sacrifice.

Before anyone concludes I'm promoting Judaism, remember the four classifications of the Law mentioned in the beginning of this chapter: the moral law, the ceremonial law, the civil law, and the dietary restrictions. It is extremely important to understand the significance of each of these categories. Christianity never abolished the moral law of God, for these never change. They are the essence of God: complete moral purity. They existed before the Mosaic Law was given at Sinai. However, the ceremonial, civil, and dietary laws were a covenant agreement God made with Israel only. Some of these laws were simply rules that made a unique distinction between the nation Israel and the other nations. This distinction is still obvious after thirty-five hundred years since its origination. Christ, the fulfiller of the Law, made allowances regarding certain requirements of the Law. He showed by example that some laws could and should be abolished: He ate without ceremoniously washing his hands; He described David as lawfully eating from the bread in The Tabernacle, something forbidden by the ceremonial law; He healed on the sabbath. Furthermore, both the apostles Peter and Paul—assigned leaders of the Jewish and Gentile churches respectively—made it clear in their writings that Christians were not obligated to follow the ceremonial, civil, and dietary regulations of the Law. They specifically challenged the Jewish Christians who drew attention to the works of the Law as an addition for salvation. Circumcision was no longer necessary for salvation; rather, one is saved because the sacrifice of Christ cuts away the sin that clings to us. Observing holy days is not necessary for salvation; however, one should attempt to live according to the moral guidelines of the holy God. The Gentile Christians in the first church were not obligated to observe the Jewish Passover, but participation in the Christian sacrament of Communion was encouraged. Still, observing Communion did not bring salvation, nor was it a perquisite for salvation; participating in Christian Communion reminded the believer of the horrendous manner in which Christ purchased salvation.

The moral obligations encompassed in the Ten Commandments have never been rescinded, but Jesus fine-tuned the ten into two commandments: love the Lord with all your heart and love your neighbor as yourself. Confusion happens when some confuse the teaching of Paul regarding the works of the Law. Paul never intended for the believer to live any way he desired, giving no attention to righteous living. To avoid any confusion as to whether or not the moral regulations woven throughout the Law were abolished, let's consider what Paul meant when he referred to the works of the Law. This terminology had a specific meaning that has lost focus because we don't understand its origination. The translating of the Dead Sea scrolls has shed light on what was heretofore an assumed understanding of the meaning of this terminology. According to author Martin Abegg , the phrase in the New Testament, "works of the law," is not to be found in any other ancient writings until the translation of the Dead Sea Scrolls. He explains some of the issues that may have surfaced among the Jewish Christians as being described by Paul as "works of the law."[1] Ancient writers used this common first century terminology with full understanding as to the meaning and therefore did not elaborate as to specifics. Since they omitted specifics, some have improperly interposed their meaning, primarily suggesting that the Christian is saved by grace and therefore has no restrictions as to how to live. This is a very loose interpretation and certainly overlooks a host of Scriptures that give specifics as to how the Christian should live. When the New Testament writers explained that works does not save us, they were not suggesting we should give little or no attention to how we live. They were making a generalized reference to the civil, dietary, and ceremonial regulations of the Law. In short, none of these can save us.

We can now ascertain that the authors of the New Testament—in their reference to works—were not referring to moral issues included in the Law, sometimes called works of righteousness; rather, the works they referred to related to civil, dietary, and more specifically to the Jewish temple ceremonies. The Essenes, who inhabited Qumran (where the Dead Sea Scrolls were found and who were the transcribers of the scrolls), felt the priests in Jerusalem performed the ceremonial worship in an unholy manner unacceptable by the Lord. They considered these "works of the law" as insufficient for Israel's salvation. Furthermore, in surveying the entirety of Paul's Epistles, he certainly addressed specific issues that he considered to be "works of the law." These include: circumcision, ritual sacrifices, eating of certain meats, and observance of certain feast days. These "works of the law" had not been sufficient to save mankind, nor had the Israelites been able to perfectly perform them.

The first recorded Church Council at Jerusalem, in attempting to create harmony among the Jewish and Gentile Christians, offered some restrictions that were associated with the moral laws of God, but also two that seem associated with the Jewish dietary laws (abstaining from things strangled and from blood—perhaps one and the same in meaning). Upon further examination, though the rules regarding eating of blood may have seemed silly to the Gentiles, they actually predated the Mosaic Law, and the Gentile world was privy to how offensive this was to the Jewish people. God gave such restrictions to Noah after the flood but before the Mosaic Law (Genesis 9:4). However, in the apostles' decision to request that the Gentile church observe this Old Covenant tradition, the guidelines were not associated with salvation; rather, the Gentile Christians were demanded to observe these guidelines to avoid offending the Jewish Christians and bringing disharmony within the Christian community. The council also acknowledged that some of the "works of the law" were too difficult for even the Jews to obey. Still, the council demanded of the Gentile church observance of certain moral laws of the Old Covenant, mainly refraining from idolatry and fornication: major practices of the Gentiles. This does not limit our moral teachings to avoiding only two sins; rather, these were major issues and therefore highlighted. Nothing was mentioned about stealing, or killing, or lying. Evidently, these were not controversial issues and needed not to be addressed.

> And the apostles and elders came together for to consider of this matter. And when there had been much disputing, Peter rose up, and said unto them, Men and brethren, ye know how that a good while ago God made choice among us, that the Gentiles by my mouth should hear the word of the gospel, and believe. And God, which knoweth the hearts, bare them witness, giving them the Holy Ghost, even as he did unto us; And put no difference between us and them, purifying their hearts by faith. Now therefore why tempt ye God, to put a yoke upon the neck of the disciples, which neither our fathers nor we were able to bear? But we believe that through the grace of the Lord Jesus Christ we shall be saved, even as they.
>
> Acts 15:6-11

> Wherefore my sentence is, that we trouble not them, which from among the Gentiles are turned to God: But that we write unto them, that they abstain from pollutions of idols, and from fornication, and from things strangled, and from blood. For Moses of old time hath in every city them that preach him, being read in the synagogues every sabbath day.
>
> Acts 15:9-21

From this council there are a number of observations we should consider:
- The Jewish Christians were not saved because of obedience

to the Law, for if that had been the case, Christ's sacrifice would have been unnecessary. Further, the Gentiles, who lived apart from the Law, were given salvation through faith in Christ's atoning sacrifice (Acts 15:8-9).

- Even the Jewish people had not been totally obedient to the whole law (Acts 15:10).
- We are saved, not by the Law, but by the grace of the Lord Jesus Christ (Acts 15:11).
- Certain restrictions, however, were applied (Acts 15:20).
- Monotheistic restrictions were from the Ten Commandments, or the moral law, while other restrictions can be considered as being from the civil, or ceremonial law (Acts 15:20), though we pointed out earlier the requirement regarding eating of blood was a restriction given to Noah long before the nation Israel entered into a covenant relationship with God.
- The Apostles sought guidance, not only from the Holy Scripture, but also through prayer (Acts 15:28).
- They determined not to place upon the Gentiles burdensome regulations of the Law deemed unnecessary for salvation (Acts 15:28).
- They asked the Gentile church to observe a few cardinal restrictions in order to continue in harmony and fellowship with the Jewish church (Acts 15:28).

These observations offer guidelines for us to follow today. They leave room for the church to evaluate and determine when and what changes need to be made in order to prevent unnecessary burdens upon converts. At the same time, these observations allow for the church to determine certain restrictions and requirements can be placed upon converts. I personally believe some restrictions are important because of the church's responsibility to move in the direction of righteousness versus following the pattern of the world. In an editorial, Kathleen Parker of the Washington Post explains why society has become more tolerant of deviant and boorish behavior. We have taken the path of " . . . normalizing the deviant to accommodate our moral decay."[2] The church dare not follow this pattern. To remain the "light on a hill" and the "salt of the earth" we must be constant and cautious in our dealing with change.

Conservative churches (those maintaining a high set of standards for parishioners) must be careful not to refuse change simply for the sake of being able to boast, "We have not changed." Such an attitude places them in constant danger of defaulting toward Pharisaism and hypocrisy—blind self-righteousness and cloaking one's faults by excessive acts of goodness. It is necessary for any conservative movement, no matter how sincere, to constantly align (both outward acts of right living and inner attitudes regarding one's fellowman) the heart and mind with the heart and mind of Christ.

Change is frightening, for change opens and closes doors, tears down old fences, and builds new. In doing such we dare not compromise righteous living as established by Scripture. Still, cultural changes are in constant motion, not necessarily for the best. We must contend with cultural change, for the church has been changing since its conception. We must not allow fears to immobilize us from necessary change, but we should always consider change with much prayer, counsel, and study of Scripture.

I believe the Scripture is clear enough for us to take a strong stand for righteousness. The concern lies in whether or not the pulpit is up to the task of challenging society's norms. Few want to be branded intolerant, but the Scripture is never tolerant toward sin. The Scripture offers forgiveness, but also demands change. Jesus proclaimed to the adulterous woman, " . . . go, and sin no more" (John 8:11). The church must maintain a clear vision regarding biblical morality. However, we must also be able to scripturally qualify right and wrong in our society. A cultural change isn't necessarily wrong simply because we didn't endorse it in the past. Further, to say that change has not taken place in the church the past fifty years is to shut our eyes to reality. Society (including the church) endorsed beards and mustaches as being a sign of masculinity in the early part of the twentieth century, but some churches associated the same with the rebellion of the hippy movement during the 60's and 70's and therefore placed certain restrictions on facial hair on men. Now, some want to challenge the teaching, explaining facial hair on men is no longer a sign of rebellion and therefore it isn't necessary for the church to teach against men wearing beards. Others insist we simply cannot change a teaching because "that's been our teaching for fifty years." Consider the length of ladies dresses from the early 1900's to the present. The length of Christian ladies' dresses has definitely become shorter, which is change. I am not advocating any particular change (For clarification of my personal beliefs, I'd advocate for us to go in the direction of longer versus shorter.); rather, I'm simply making an observation that we do make adjustments in each generation. However, there are principles of the Law of God that never change—modesty for example—and to forsake the teaching of modesty is to always error. Therefore, though the style, and certainly the length, of clothing have gone through much change, we must establish guidelines that promote modesty; moreover, the church must define modesty instead of allowing the present trend of society to do so. Why modesty? It speaks of betrothal to one's spouse, and for the Christian, betrothal to God. Modesty tends to balance a world gone mad with outlandish and provocative dress. Indecent dress facilitates lust (but never excuses such), so why would any Christian choose to dress provocative? And the Bible demands attention regarding modesty and moderateness. The pulpit has the right, and the responsibility, to establish a benchmark for such. This is not suggesting salvation comes through "the works of the law." It is directing us as Christians to live in accordance with New Testament teaching regarding responsibility as a representative of Christ in a decadent society. We dare not "normalize the deviant to accommodate our moral decay."

What we must define is the difference between the "works of the law" and the "works of righteousness." While the majority of the "works of the law" were not incorporated into the teachings of the Gentile church and therefore they are not an issue within the Gentile church, New Testament writers demanded that "works of righteousness" be manifest by all believers, though I believe the writers demonstrated patience and love in their demands and reprimands. The "works of the Law" cannot save us; however, under the Old Covenant they were a pattern to Israel of the coming Savior. In retrospect we realize salvation comes only through the grace of God made possible at Calvary. Yet, when God's grace engages our lives, we are immediately challenged to follow after (not the "works of the law") the "works of righteousness," which can be found in the moral law recorded by Moses, the moral principles of the patriarchs and the prophets, and the New Testament writers. Further, these "works of righteousness" have never been rescinded in the Scripture and must never be done away with by Christians. Further, we must understand that we are still not saved by our works of righteousness; rather, we manifest right living because God's grace saved us through Christ's sacrificial death at Calvary. We desire and follow after right living out of a grateful heart. Christ's abiding grace continues to work in our lives, transforming us more and more into His likeness.

So, whatever happened to the Law? It did it's job. As a schoolmaster it brought us to Christ. It showed us our sinful state, for at our best in attempting to follow the Law we still came up short; moreover, it showed us that obeying the rules and requirements of a holy God cannot save us. Our fallen nature always defaults to carnality, and we can never please Him by our personal righteousness. So, from the beginning of creation, God created a perfect plan for mankind's redemption. That plan unfolded throughout the Old Testament, including the giving of the Law to the covenant people, Israel. With the passing of time, they rejected both God and His ways, silencing the prophet with imprisonment, punishment, and death. In order to contain His wrath, for four hundred years, God withdrew from Israel and silence prevailed among God's people as the prophetic utterances ceased in the temple and synagogues. The teachers of the Law used this absence of God's influence for personal gain and control over the populace. Then, John, the thundering Baptist, breaks upon the scene with two messages. The first message was a call to repentance. Repent, you religious ruling rabbis, who think you've mastered the Law, but mock it because what you profess on the outside is opposite of what is in your hearts. Repent, because outwardly you look righteous, for you purposely obey the minute details of the Law for show and personal gain, but within, your hearts do not resemble the heart of God which is full of compassion, love, and mercy. The first sermon infuriated the religious leaders; the second sermon frightened them. This message proclaimed that one was coming who would not merely tell how to live, but He would guide by example, and He would assist in righteous living, for He would live inside the believer in the joy and strength of the Holy Spirit.

When Jesus stepped upon the scene, John defined Him as the Lamb of God that takes away the sins of the world. Jesus' message fine-tuned His purpose, not to do away with the Law, but to fulfill it. He did so by dying on the cross as the perfect human sacrifice. The lack of such a sacrifice had rendered the Law incomplete. Further, Jesus didn't just excuse our sins; His sinless life, dying as a sinner deserves, paid our debt of sin. God could have pardoned our sin, but He chose to do something more awesome: He paid for our sins with His own life. And what did that do to the Law? It completed it. As the breath of life exited His lips, Jesus proclaimed, "It is finished." Not, "I am defeated", but rather, "It is done. Victory is won! Salvation is possible! The debt of sin is paid! Sinners can now become saints!" The law of grace no more condemns us to hell, but compels us to seek the Savior. Savior seekers are not namby-pambies who hide sinful living behind the skirt of grace; rather, they realize their breaking of God's laws of righteousness also breaks God's heart. Savior seekers seek grace to cover their sins, but also grace to live righteous. That was the intention of the Old Testament Law, but it lacked the motivating love and power of a Savior Who was both human and Divine.

In Christ, sin tempted Deity, but Christ never succumbed to the temptation. Since Deity condemned all sinners to the ultimate penalty of death and hell, because of the death of the sinless Christ, death and hell became the debtor. The sinless, but condemned and crucified, God/man applied His unjust death to the sinners' debt. The result? A fallen creation was miraculously restored to favor with their Creator.

Chapter 6

HOW AM I TO LIVE UNDER GRACE

Some want to totally abandon the Old Testament, but to do so would create a vacuum—not only in the morality of our world, but also in our legal and social system—that could easily be filled with debauchery. How then should we address the Old Testament, specifically the Mosaic Law? We must approach the Old Testament in light of the teachings of the New Testament. When we do this, we not only maintain the moral teaching of the Scripture, but we strengthen such. Also, when we harmonize the Old Testament with the teachings of Christ and the writings of the Apostles, we realize the sacrificial system of the Old Testament, along with the observance of certain days and feasts, are no longer applicable regarding salvation. These are significant only if they can find meaning through the New Testament teaching. Consider how the New Testament writers incorporated the principles of the Old Testament teachings into Christian observances: feasts—such as Passover and Pentecost—took on Christian meaning in observing communion and experiencing the baptism of the Holy Spirit. Further, rituals (such as circumcision), became merely symbolic instead of literal, and took on a spiritual significance in the necessity of having our sinful nature cut away by the New Birth.

The Old Testament Passover Feast was an annual Jewish celebration commemorating their deliverance from four hundred years of Egyptian bondage. The first Passover established a new beginning for Israel, and the month marked the beginning of a New Year and new life made possible by the mighty hand of their God. The Jewish Passover finds Christian meaning in the crucifixion, for Christ became our Passover lamb, and the Christian observance of Communion is a replication of the Jewish Passover.

> Purge out therefore the old leaven, that ye may be a new lump, as ye are unleavened. For even Christ our Passover is sacrificed for us: Therefore let us keep the feast, not with old leaven, neither with the leaven of malice and wickedness; but with the unleavened bread of sincerity and truth.
>
> I Corinthians 5:7-8

The Jewish Passover commemorated the death angel of God passing over their homes in Egypt, sparing their firstborn, while the Egyptian's first born suffered death. When we partake of Communion we are testifying to our release from the bondage and consequence of sin. For the Christian, Communion commemorates how Christ's death purchased new life for all who would accept His sacrifice. The acts of Communion (eating the bread and drinking the fruit of the vine) acknowledge the means of this new way of life: the crucifixion of our Lord.

> For he hath made him to be sin for us, who knew no sin; that we might be made the righteousness of God in him.
>
> II Corinthians 5:21

Jesus' last meal with His disciples—prior to the crucifixion—was the Passover Feast. During that meal, which we refer to as the Lord's Supper, Christ revealed they had entered into a New Covenant and He was the New Covenant (New Testament) Passover lamb. We commemorate the crucifixion, not by participating in The Passover but through partaking of Christian Communion.

> And as they were eating, Jesus took bread, and bless-
> ed it, and brake it, and gave it to the disciples, and
> said, Take, eat; this is my body. And he took the cup,
> and gave thanks, and gave it to them, saying, Drink
> ye all of it; For this is my blood of the new testament,
> which is shed for many for the remission of sins. But I
> say unto you, I will not drink henceforth of this fruit
> of the vine, until that day when I drink it new with
> you in my Father's kingdom.
>
>   Matthew 26:26-29

The Jewish Feast of Pentecost finds Christian meaning in the observance of the outpouring of the Holy Spirit and the birthday of the church. Further, the personal infilling of the Holy Spirit is the partaking of a Christian Pentecost. The original feast commemorat-ed both the giving of the Law and thanksgiving for the harvest. For the Christian, Pentecost is the writing of the Law of God upon our hearts—a heart change instead of mere head knowledge. Paul ex-pressed, "Forasmuch as ye are manifestly declared to be the epistle of Christ ministered by us, written not with ink, but with the Spirit of the living God; not in tables of stone, but in fleshy tables of the heart" (II Corinthians 3:3). Further, Christ was the bread of life come down for us from heaven. No wonder the psalmist wrote, "O taste and see that the Lord is good: blessed is the man that trusteth in him" (Psalms 34:8). Salvation wasn't a random act; rather, God followed a well thought-out plan. Christ was crucified during the Jewish Pass-over Feast, and the Holy Spirit was specifically outpoured on the Jewish Feast of Pentecost. In the New Birth experience the Christian readily understands the concept of Christ coming to fulfill the Law.

> And when the day of Pentecost was fully come, they
> were all with one accord in one place. And sudden-
> ly there came a sound from heaven as of a rushing

mighty wind, and it filled all the house where they were sitting. And there appeared unto them cloven tongues like as of fire, and it sat upon each of them. And they were all filled with the Holy Ghost, and began to speak with other tongues, as the Spirit gave them utterance.

Acts 2:1-4

The Christian doesn't merely commemorate Pentecost; he experiences Pentecost as Christ enters into the believer. The Law becomes alive on the inside, rather than a burdensome and constant stumbling block on his pathway. The bread of heaven is consumed instead of celebrated, and the command for obedience is made possible by the indwelling power of the Holy Spirit.

Circumcision of the male on the eight day after birth is a Jewish act of obeying the covenant first made between God and Abraham and later included in the covenant with Israel through the Mosaic Law. For the Christian, circumcision is no longer a physical act but a spiritual experience of the heart. Originally, it was a physical act man did out of submission to his covenant with God. In the New Covenant it became something God did for man: the cutting away of sin.

In whom also ye are circumcised with the circumcision made without hands, in putting off the body of the sins of the flesh by the circumcision of Christ: Buried with him in baptism, wherein also ye are risen with him through the faith of the operation of God, who hath raised him from the dead. And you, being dead in your sins and the uncircumcision of your flesh, hath he quickened together with him, having forgiven you all trespasses; Blotting out the handwriting of ordinances that was against us, which was contrary to us, and took it out of the way, nailing it to his cross;.

Colossians 2:11-14

We find much of the principles of the Old Testament Moral Law in the teachings of the New Testament. Jesus' teaching to love your neighbor as yourself is a direct quote from Leviticus 19:18. Though I am quick to point out that salvation comes through Jesus Christ alone, the Old Testament teachings are still very relevant for the Christian life.

Jesus did not discard the teachings of the Law; rather, He explained and refined them by His teachings. Typical of this refining is His Sermon on the Mount. Quoting from various Old Testament Scriptures, He redefined—in contrast to the current trend of Jewish religious leaders—what it meant to love God with all your heart and your neighbor as yourself. Even a child schooled in the local synagogue, could understand His teaching: "Blessed are the poor . . . they that mourn . . . the meek . . . they which do hunger and thirst . . . the merciful . . . the pure in heart . . . the peacemakers . . . ." One writer expressed, adult rules are basically an expression of what we learned in kindergarten. As an adult, it's no longer necessary for us to follow every rule we did in kindergarten, like holding hands as we cross the street, but the same principle must be applied: always extending a hand to someone in need. If we lived our adult life according to the principles we learned in kindergarten, the world would be a much better place. Conversely, as we grow older, our Adamic nature becomes more consuming. That is why we dare not abandon the principles of the Old Testament. Further, that is why we must partake of the New Birth; we need the Holy Spirit to subdue the old nature. The Law merely clarified the rules; it did not enable one to obey the rules. The means of obedience was the fear of consequences, which generally works best when someone is watching. The New Testament clarifies which of the Old Testament Laws are necessary to please God, and it offers the believer the power to stop sinning—against God and our fellow man—through the indwelling Spirit subduing the old nature and resetting the default mode from carnality to spirituality.

Knowing which of the Old Testament Laws, if any, we should obey causes some confusion: what food to eat, what rituals to participate in or to abandon, what customs to follow. How can we know what to obey? In order to properly answer this question, we must give attention to the four previously mentioned classifications of the Law: moral, ceremonial, civil, and dietary. The moral laws of God are associated with His holiness; therefore, the moral laws of God never change. Some regulations in the ceremonial laws were mere typologies—not the real thing—and were therefore subject to ceasing once the real thing came. Further, many of these requirements were not linked to morality; conversely, they were guidelines for compatibility with one's fellowman. Some rules regulated sanitation guidelines for as many as five million Israelites camping out for forty years. These may not fully apply to a more advanced society with proper sanitation and refrigeration; however, the principles should remain—they may be great rules to abide by, but they have nothing to do with salvation. Further, the Mosaic Law was a covenant between God and the nation Israel. With this in mind, we can readily see that the Gentile church was not obligated to follow all the rules and regulations of the Old Testament; still, even nature itself teaches us the significance of some of the principles required by a holy God that were recorded in the Law. For the sake of clarification, let's place all of the Mosaic Law into one of three groups.

Let's label the first group "done away with." This group served a purpose in the in the Old Testament as a symbol of something that was to come. We can cease following these because Jesus Christ brought something better than the symbolic. This "done away with" group does not necessarily mean it was never important, but it was a mere symbol of something to come that was far better. Like a roadmap, the symbols pointed the way, but once we have arrived at our destiny, we no longer need to stare at the map. Once we've experienced salvation, we no longer need to give attention to the symbolic (the feasts and rituals of the Law that guided the Israelites through the Old Covenant and into the New Covenant). The writer of Hebrews shares a list of blessings given in the New Covenant that are much better than the old: better revelation, better hope, better priesthood, better covenant, better promises, better sacrifices, better possessions, better country, and better resurrection. In the "done away with" group we find laws regulating the priesthood, sacrifices and offerings, feasts and holy days, dietary restrictions, religious purification, certain capital punishments, the eating of clean and unclean animals, the eye for an eye concept, and numerous other general regulations. Under the New Covenant these all must be interpreted in light of salvation through Christ.

Let's label the second group "still to be obeyed." Multiple sources affirm this group as moral commandments of the Creator: they preceded the writing of the Mosaic Law, were upheld by the prophets, and were reinforced by New Testament writings. We continue to obey these commands because Jesus, the apostles, and various New Testament writers taught us to do so. Because of this category, Christians should be cautious in their attitude regarding "freedom from the Law," commonly referred to by some as "Christian liberty." Too many misinterpret Paul's writings regarding liberty in Christ. The summation of some misinterpretations goes something like this: "Christ set us free from our sins so we are free to commit those same sins without feeling guilty." Something doesn't ring true in this statement, especially when compared with a host of New Testament Scriptures regarding right living.

Consider the biblical meaning of Christian liberty. First, we are free from the eternal consequences of repented sins: our debt of sin was paid by Christ's atoning death, is no longer held to our charge, and will not be permissible evidence against us at our eternal judgment. Second, we are free from the bondage of sin's devastating grip upon our lives. We now have the indwelling power to break the yoke of sin that formally bound and controlled us. This is not to suggest we never sin, but it is to understand we are not dominated by sin. Further, our attitude about sin has changed: we no longer take pleasure in sin, for we recognize the displeasure sin brings to Jesus Christ. Through Christ's grace we find the will to overcome sinful actions: we can now override our carnal default mode.

Christian freedom has a unique twist. Though delivered from a carnal taskmaster—Satan and our sinful nature—we are still servants. We had not the personal ability to set ourselves free from sin: we had to have a deliverer. Since someone else won our freedom from sin, such freedom automatically makes us a servant to that someone and something else: Christ and righteousness. The Scripture uses Israel's deliverance from Egyptian bondage as a typology of the Christian's deliverance from sin. The Egyptian Empire dominated Israel's every waking moment. Their deliverance came only because Jehovah—directing and empowering His servant Moses—overthrew the gods and Pharaoh that enslaved them. The Scripture explains, " . . . the mighty hand, and the stretched out arm, whereby the Lord thy

God brought thee out . . . " (Deuteronomy 7:19). Jehovah broke the arm of the mighty Egyptian Empire that held Israel in slavery, and the conqueror gets the spoils. The result of God delivering Israel was a covenant relationship between Israel and their new master: Jehovah.

The Old Testament Law defined the covenant relationship between Jehovah and Israel, but Israel continually broke the covenant. In retrospect, the New Testament (specifically the book of Hebrews) describes the covenant as being a yoke of bondage that lacked a perfect sacrifice and lacked the power to remove sin and the guilt that it brought. Further, The Law lacked the power of an indwelling Savior to overcome sin. "For the law made nothing perfect, but the bringing in of a better hope did; by the which we draw nigh unto God" (Hebrews 7:19). The Law pointed toward the Savior. In the Book of Leviticus, the key words are "access" (to God's presence by atonement through sacrifices) and "holiness" (which occurs over eighty times in Leviticus and deals with the way of living in God's presence). Since the laws of the Old Testament were full of the right way for men and women to live, it should not surprise us that many of those laws were carried over into the New Testament. The list includes regulations regarding many areas: marriage, caring for the poor, differentiation of the sexes, witchcraft, immorality, honoring of elders, respect for parents, treatment of strangers, fairness, idolatry, vows, giving, and numerous other regulations. Christianity never abolished the righteous principles of the Law; in some cases the New Covenant elevated the bar. The superiority of the New Testament over the Old Testament is in the sacrificial Lamb planned by God to remove sin, and the indwelling Holy Spirit to sanctify and empower the believer. With this New Covenant plan there remains responsibilities. So, this second category of laws we classify as "still need to be obeyed," but we now have the means to do so.

Let's label the third group as the "not sure what to do with these" group. This group, however, has nothing to do with obtaining salvation; rather, they are guidelines associated with daily living within an imperfect world outside of the Garden of Eden. Since we are not sure how to apply all these regulations, we should be cautious about placing them as absolutes, and also cautious in disregarding them. An example within the "not sure what to do with these" category could be a hosts of detailed regulations regarding personal hygiene in order to avoid diseases. Though this category is absolutely unlinked to salvation requirements, some of the regulations seem wise guidelines to follow, and we follow many of these guidelines without realizing we are obeying a requirement of the Law. Since the New Testament is silent on much of the minute details contained within the Law, we are unsure as to which of these we should follow, but the New Testament is not silent regarding how we are saved: only through Christ. Obeying a thousand rules doesn't bring a moment of salvation, but the New Birth through Christ brings salvation in a moment. And once saved from sin, one should desire right living apart from sin. Because we are saved through Christ, we desire to live a live pleasing to Him.

Two reasons prompt the Christian to give consideration to the Law. One, it holds "a shadow of good things to come," primarily, the significance of atonement for sins. Under the Law the atoning blood of sacrificial animals was essential for Israel to maintain their covenant relationship with God; likewise, under the New Covenant, the sacrifice that Jesus Christ made as a once-for-all-time offering for sin is essential for us to have a saving relationship with God. "And almost all things are by the law purged with blood; and without shedding of blood is no remission" (Hebrews 9:22). Atonement for sin under the Law came only by the shedding of the blood of an innocent animal (and this only postponed dealing with the sin); we find atonement only through Christ's death applied to our lives. There is no other way for mortal man's sins to be paid.

The second reason we should give consideration to the Law is to recognize God's call to righteous living. The old covenant focused upon the holiness of God; likewise, the New Covenant directs us toward the holiness of God and us pursuing a life of righteousness. "Be ye holy; for I am holy" (I Peter 1:16). We must recognize holiness cannot be produced through mortal means; it comes only through the atoning blood of Jesus Christ applied to our lives. Paul emphasized this several times in his writings, that righteousness is not through the works of the Law. This is what Paul meant when he wrote to the Roman church, "For Christ is the end of the law for righteousness to every one that believeth" (Romans 10:4).

Contrary to the loose interpretation of some regarding grace, we dare not overlook the numerous teachings of the New Testament regarding how we ought to live after we attain the righteousness of Christ through faith. Further, when we sin, no good deed can erase the sin; rather, only the atonement of Christ's blood can compensate for sin. We must again confess sin and through faith accept the application of Christ's blood to remove our sin. Acquisition of forgiveness is not an automatic withdrawal from the reserves of grace; rather, we must request the application by faith in Christ's Word. To request forgiveness acknowledges several important matters: sin separates us from God; there are consequences of sin; only Christ's atoning blood can remove sin. "If we confess our sins, he is faithful and just to forgive us our sins, and to cleanse us from all unrighteousness" (I John 1:9). This Scripture is not to trivialize the importance of right living. The fact that forgiveness is always possible through Christ should never minimize our efforts to please Christ by the way we live; conversely, we are commanded by Scripture to live holy. This commandment covers two areas of commitment: separation "unto God" and separation "from the world of sin." We are called into fellowship with Christ, and we are called unto separation from the ungodliness of the world. The call to separation from the world is not to promote legalism (a strict adherence to a list of rules), but it is a call to obey the Word of God. As we cringe at the concerns regarding legalism (a justifiable concern, for legalism can well be self-righteousness, which God hates), let's not fall into the opposite trap of antinomianism—grace as a lollypop for self-centeredness—which is carnality at its worst. While legalist cast guilt by overbearing restraints, antinomians purposely live without restraints, suggesting this makes grace abound—grace does abound, but there is a limit to abounding grace. The New Testament writers had to combat this boundless grace philosophy, which basically taught, since we're saved by grace, live any way you want—as sinful as you want—for the grace of God saves you, and the more sinful you live, the more awesome God's grace becomes for you. This blatant false teaching regarding grace existed in the first church, and Paul confronted it in his letters to the churches. His letters to the Roman church is quite clear regarding the misuse of grace to cloak willful unrighteous living. "What shall we say then? Shall we continue in sin, that grace may abound? God forbid. How shall we, that are dead to sin, live any longer therein?" (Romans 6:1-2). When concerned that salvation through grace might be marginalized through zealous works of righteousness, we must ask the right questions regarding salvation. Perhaps this simple analogy will help.

> Question: Can a man get saved on his way to see a dirty movie? The answer is yes. How can he be saved in such a carnal state of mind? The work of grace! But the analogy doesn't end here. Too few only ask this first question, and therefore fail to mature in Christ, fulfilling the biblical directive to "grow in grace." There is another question we should ask. It is similar, but the slight difference evokes a far better understanding of grace. The antinomians avoid this question: Should a man who gets saved on his way to a see a dirty movie continue on his way to view the dirty movie? Perhaps I am being overly simplistic, but it is significant to consider what grace saves us from: sin. An innocent child—who has never experienced the New Birth—will not be cast into hell merely because he possesses the sinful nature of Adam. He doesn't fall into condemnation until such a time as he is aware of right and wrong, and he becomes maturely responsible for making choices regarding such. The sinful nature will someday motivate this same innocent child to choose to commit sin. At such time God will view him as a sinner. That's when grace kicks in and offers salvation. And so, the man on his way to view a dirty movie is detained and remade into a saint. Grace isn't finished; it has just begun its work. Grace doesn't say, "You're now saved, so don't worry about whether or not you commit future sins." Instead, grace says, "Since your sins made you a sinner, and the consequence of your sinful lifestyle nailed the Savior to a cross, don't you want to stop committing those sins?" To live otherwise is to distort the beautiful message of grace; more so, it is a mockery to grace.

Ironically, the idea of going easy on sin isn't coming from unbelievers, but such ideas come from pews, and worse still, from pulpits. The world understands it is in bondage to sinful habits, pleasures, and fleshly lusts. The sinner wants freedom from the guilt associated with sin, but he also wants freedom from the sin. Christ died that we might be set free from the guilt but also free from continuing in sinful habits. Antinomians—contrary to Paul's outcry against continuing in sin—condemn the pulpits that attempt to identify morality, modesty, and the things God considers a holy lifestyle. They often consider this legalism. They condemn such teachings as trying to earn salvation through good works. Though many legalists exists, it is an over exaggeration to say that teaching against unrighteous living is legalism.

Still, not all rules of the Old Covenant are necessary for the Christian. The Law included rules of separation—identifying the Israelites as being in a unique relationship with God, in contrast to other nations—which Christ and the New Testament writers clarified as unassociated with righteousness but were merely associated with identifying Israel as a nation set apart for Jehovah. To insist the Christian community must follow such rules is often legalistic. At the same time, the Law identified certain rules as being a part of the morality of God. These rules contrast the sinful nature of mankind, and identify his sinful condition, directing him to look to God for salvation. Likewise, our message today needs to identify sins so that man will see his need for a Savior, understand that the Savior paid the debt for sin, and recognize salvation comes only through Christ. Experiencing the New Birth removes our sin and guilt, and Christ's indwelling Spirit produces a regenerated heart that seeks to turn from sin. The message of grace unlimited—telling me not to try too hard, for I can't stop sinning anyway—encourages spiritual immaturity, irresponsible, and unfruitful living. Following this loose interpretation of grace dissuades righteousness, which Christ loves, and it promotes worldliness, which He hates. Following worldliness will consume energy, time, and talents. Such a lifestyle is insulting to our holy God, and such a standard of living is a disappointment to our suffering Savior. Tragically, the message of grace taught in the Bible, and the message coming across many pulpits today, sound incompatible. We should herald the message of grace, God's love, and forgiveness. At the same time, we should not omit the message of the Scripture that pleads for separation from sin. We should consider all Scriptures that challenge a slothfulness regarding sin, and we should balance them with the Scriptures that speak to us about the grace of God.

Love not the world, neither the things that are in the world. If any man love the world, the love of the Father is not in him. For all that is in the world, the lust of the flesh, and the lust of the eyes, and the pride of life, is not of the Father, but is of the world. And the world passeth away, and the lust thereof: but he that doeth the will of God abideth for ever.

I John 2:15-17

Mortify therefore your members which are upon the earth; fornication, uncleanness, inordinate affection, evil concupiscence, and covetousness, which is idolatry: For which things' sake the wrath of God cometh on the children of disobedience: In the which ye also walked some time, when ye lived in them. But now ye also put off all these; anger, wrath, malice, blasphemy, filthy communication out of your mouth. Lie not one to another, seeing that ye have put off the old man with his deeds; And have put on the new man, which is renewed in knowledge after the image of him that created him:

Colossians 3:5-10

And they that are Christ's have crucified the flesh with the affections and lusts. But God forbid that I should glory, save in the cross of our Lord Jesus Christ, by whom the world is crucified unto me, and I unto the world.

Galatians 5:24; 6:14

Consider how one commentator explains Galatians 6:14:

> The cross of Christ, representing the horrible death that the Savior suffered for our eternal salvation, is now the barrier by which the world is fenced off from us and us from the world. The "world" means everything that is opposed to God, His kingdom, and His righteousness. 1) For those who make the cross their life, their glory, and their boast, the world with all its accepted standards, values, opinions, honors, and lifestyles is no longer cherished or loved. 2) For us to be "crucified with Christ" includes our being crucified to the world. There is no sharing in the salvation and glory of His cross without turning our backs on all the earthly pleasures that draw our hearts away from Christ and His nearness.[1]

How then am I to live under the message of grace? Am I exempt from the laws of God simply because they are from the Old Testament? It is not placement of Scripture that is significant (Old or New Testament); rather, it is purpose that is significant. I am exempt only from those laws for which Christ and the New Testament writers offered exemption—either explicitly or by implication. Why should I justify following after the world by arguing that I am living under grace? Yes, the grace of God has set me free from the guilt and consequences of sin, but grace has not set me free to continue in sin with little or no effort to stop sinning. Rather, God's grace has set me free from my sins, and God's love calls me into a deeper relationship with Christ as Savior, where I attempt to live apart from sin. If I sin out of weakness—which is a constant threat—I am not without a remedy for sin. In Christ I no longer sin out of wickedness—for Christ has given me a new nature. I may sin out of weakness (giving in to the old nature that remains a part of me until the rapture), but I will fight such weakness and will be quick to repent (instead of making excuse for my sin) when I fail. Grace leads me to repentance instead of pretense. "If we say that we have no sin, we deceive ourselves, and the truth is not in us. If we confess our sins, he is faithful and just to forgive us our sins, and to cleanse us from all unrighteousness. If we say that we have not sinned, we make him a liar, and his word is not in us" (I John 1:8-10).

God's initial act of grace in our lives brings us salvation, but the journey to heaven has only begun. Grace walks with us along the way. Though Christ has called us to live above sin, the Christian is in constant threat of sin, and too often yields to temptation, but grace still abounds if we fail, and grace calls us to repentance. Our confession of sin, and request for forgiveness, continues to activate God's grace to forgive our sins. This process of the Holy Spirit working within us is called sanctification. Just as our former sins were justified by the act of God on Calvary's tree, our current sins are removed by the work of God in our lives through the continual process of sanctification. Just as the initial act of grace required our obedient faith toward the New Birth, the continual act of grace in our lives requires our continual exercising of faith, repentance, and obedience. Initial justification took an initial effort on our part; likewise, continual sanctification takes continual effort on our part: both are the work of grace, and both are activated by faith and obedience. In justification we become babes in Christ by the New Birth. We stand justified, even though we are weak and limited in understanding, and our ability to please Christ is immature. This is an initial act of God. Then comes the work of the indwelling Spirit to help us attain to Christian maturity. "My little children, these things write I unto you, that ye sin not. And if any man sin, we have an advocate with the Father, Jesus Christ the righteous: And he is the propitiation for our sins: and not for ours only, but also for the sins of the whole world" (I John 2:1-2). This is the continual work of grace.

To understand that salvation only comes through Christ, and to further understand that all Christians have biblical responsibilities, is to truly understand the message of grace. The grace of God brings salvation to us as it draws us into a relationship with Christ, and it leads us into a lifestyle contrary to that of the world and Satan. The work of grace gives us a totally different attitude about sin. We may sin, but we view it as offensive to God. We are truly sorry and seek forgiveness, but we also seek change. We recognize the awful price Christ paid for our sins, and we recognize the disappointment our sin brings our Lord. Grace, that brings us salvation, is not quick to destroy us because of our weaknesses; rather, God intends to get us to heaven. He is certainly grieved when we sin, and He directs us to walk worthy of the grace He has bestowed upon us, but He is slow to anger and quick to forgive. Still, the Scripture is adamant regarding the Christian life change:

> For the grace of God that bringeth salvation hath appeared to all men, Teaching us that, denying ungodliness and worldly lusts, we should live soberly, righteously, and godly, in this present world; Looking for that blessed hope, and the glorious appearing of the great God and our Savior Jesus Christ; Who gave himself for us, that he might redeem us from all iniquity, and purify unto himself a peculiar people, zealous of good works.
>
> Titus 2:11-14

> But, beloved, remember ye the words which were spoken before of the apostles of our Lord Jesus Christ; How that they told you there should be mockers in the last time, who should walk after their own ungodly lusts. These be they who separate themselves, sensual, having not the Spirit.
>
> Jude 17-19

> I therefore, the prisoner of the Lord, beseech you that ye walk worthy of the vocation wherewith ye are called.
>
> Ephesians 4:1

> Ye are witnesses, and God also, how holily and justly and unblameably we behaved ourselves among you that believe: As ye know how we exhorted and comforted and charged every one of you, as a father doth his children. That ye would walk worthy of God, who hath called you unto his kingdom and glory.
>
> I Thessalonians 2:10-12

Paul does not accept the erroneous view of "sinning Christianity," which says that the salvation provided by Christ and His atoning blood is inadequate to save us from the bondage and power of sin, thus the Christians can sin without concern. This unbiblical doctrine maintains that all Christians must expect to sin against God often in word, thought, and deed. Contrary to the above liberal doctrine, an insightful Bible commentator explains:

> Paul affirms, with regard to his own conduct among the Thessalonians, that he behaved "holily and justly and unblameably." Paul called both the church and God Himself as witnesses that the sufficient grace of God through Christ had enabled him, as he affirmed elsewhere, to cleanse himself "from all filthiness of the flesh and spirit, perfecting holiness in the fear of God."[2]

I wonder what those who are shouting legalism today would have said against Paul. I wonder, also, how Paul's sermons would sound if he was alive today. What evils would he condemn? Would we obey him, or stone him?

PART II

FAITH

Chapter 7

WHAT IS FAITH

The New Webster's Dictionary defines faith as: " . . . complete acceptance of a truth that cannot be proven."[1] The writer of Hebrews defines faith as: " . . . the substance of things hoped for, the evidence of things not seen" (Hebrews 11:1). Another translation states: "Now faith is confidence in what we hope for and assurance about what we do not see" (Hebrews 11:1 NIV). We'll elaborate on the definition, however, pen and paper is insufficient to define faith: for faith to be effective, an individual needs to experience it.

It is one thing to know what faith is, but it is entirely something else to practice faith. As an example, we know fear by both definition and experience. There is little, if any, emotion or reaction from our definition of fear; conversely, when we experience fear (whether real or imagined), there is a host of emotions and responses that we experience. In fact, we can experience fear without having known its definition, and to experience fear is to forever be able to define it. The same is true in numerous areas: love, pain, hunger, and loneliness. Likewise, faith is a term we can discuss without having experienced it, and we can experience it prior to having a good definition. Once you have experienced faith, you can readily define it in contrast to your lack of faith. Too many know faith only by definition, but they do not possess faith.

Faith or lack thereof—whether spiritual or secular—can have both a negative and positive outlook. We may believe something bad is going to happen to us (a negative outlook), and therefore we respond by building walls in our lives that shut people and opportunities out. Our faith in the negative brought about the results we believed would come. On the other hand, we may believe life is going to treat us good (a positive outlook), and therefore we live with more openness to people and opportunities, resulting in positive things happening. Biblical faith is similar in that it is to acknowledge God even before you have experienced some tangible evidence. Faith defined by Scripture is to acknowledge that God is the Designer, Creator, and Sustainer of all life and to believe that He is looking out for the good of His creation—without being able to prove it.

Contrary to the belief of many, doubt is not the opposite of faith; it is the absence of faith. The absence of faith does not leave an indefinite void; the void is filled with questions and doubts. These left unchecked harden into unbelief, a force within itself. Jesus could do no great miracles in His hometown of Nazareth, not because they lacked faith (for He did some miracles); their unbelief resisted His ministry and so He refrained from doing great miracles. We'll talk about this later.

It is insufficient to merely define faith as believing something: even the devil believes in God, but his faith does not have a positive effect. Biblical faith is to activate in our hearts and minds a positive view of the God of Scripture: a complete acceptance of all that the Scripture says about God and His will for us, even though we cannot prove anything God's Word says nor have experienced what His Word says. Many say, "I cannot operate in faith in a God I cannot see," yet most operate daily out of a certain element of faith in the consistency of nature (something ever changing, at times chaotic and destructive). Consider, each morning when we awaken, we believe the sun will shine (even though sometimes hidden by the clouds), and we believe the day will last a full twenty-four hours. Yet we have no certain proof that this will happen. We have a past to reference, but the future is always viewed in faith, or else we would live in a constant state of fear: What if the sun doesn't rise tomorrow?

Because we believe in nature, we plan our day accordingly; however, we have no guarantee the day will endure as before. Though we have experienced this many times, there is no way of proving that this day will be like all others—we simply act upon faith in the past. Time may have proven the "what" (a twenty-four hour period of three hundred sixty-five days a year), but we cannot prove the "whether." We don't know for sure whether or not the twenty-four hour time period will continue today. This is where we operate by faith or succumb to fear. Faith becomes a choice; likewise, fear is a choice. Humans have the incredible ability for both.

Still, faith does not have to include God. The atheist can believe that tomorrow will come; of course his faith is in history: since the recording of time the sun has always risen. So, here is where the secular and the religious part. The secular may have faith in history: they believe in the future because of the past. As a Christian we have faith in God Whom we believe controls all things. We believe in the future because we believe God controlled the past; we are comforted in the present because we believe He controls the future. Can I prove this? No. That is why it is called faith.

In surveying the definition of scriptural faith, there are three points that we should consider.

Faith is Complete Acceptance

James, one of the New Testament writers, goes straight to the heart of what faith is and is not: " . . . let him ask in faith, nothing wavering. For he that wavereth is like a wave of the sea driven with the wind and tossed. For let not that man think that he shall receive anything of the Lord. But when he asks he must believe and not doubt . . . " (James 1:6-7 NIV). James was a Christian Jew, and so he well knew the history of his people regarding their Egyptian bondage. After ten undeniable miracles of the Lord, they went from four hundred years of being strangers in a foreign land (much of that in captivity) to complete deliverance from bondage, all in a matter of weeks or perhaps months. Still, they stuttered at the first hint of opposition. The Israelites failed to receive God's promises because they failed to completely accept by faith that the God who controlled the past would fulfill His promises in the future. From this example, and various other Old Testament accounts, James knew that to partially believe God is inadequate. Though Israel experienced God's deliverance through His mighty acts, these initial experiences did not guarantee them Canaan; rather, they had to persevere through faith, believing in God every day and in every situation.

Israel's failure to accept God's promises created a vacuum soon filled with doubt; doubt is the precursor of another force: unbelief. Whereas doubt leaves us unable to choose, unbelief causes us to make poor choices. Such was the case with Israel. Their unbelief resulted in rebellious acts. The Scripture likens rebellion to witchcraft; if you don't believe God can, you believe there is another force which is in control. The Israelites found themselves worshipping a golden calf (they defaulted to the gods of Egypt). For forty years they wondered in the wilderness, not allowed to enter into Canaan, all because of their unbelief. The unbelieving generation had to die out; faith had to be reborn in the younger generation.

King Saul of the Old Testament is a perfect example of allowing unbelief to dominate: believing someone other than Jehovah controlled fate. Such unbelief drove him to find a witch to call upon the departed spirit of Samuel. Interestingly, there was a time in his life when Saul destroyed witches (evidently one survived). The absence of faith allows unbelief to reign, and such non-belief is a force that creates a downward spiral away from God. You can't sit in a corner of non-belief in God's presence; you have to get in or unbelief will drive you out.

> For we are made partakers of Christ, if we hold the beginning of our confidence stedfast unto the end; While it is said, To day if ye will hear his voice, harden not your hearts, as in the provocation. For some, when they had heard, did provoke: howbeit not all that came out of Egypt by Moses. But with whom was he grieved forty years? was it not with them that had sinned, whose carcases fell in the wilderness? And to whom sware he that they should not enter into his rest, but to them that believed not? So we see that they could not enter in because of unbelief.
>
> Hebrews 3:14-19

> Let us therefore fear, lest, a promise being left us of entering into his rest, any of you should seem to come short of it. For unto us was the gospel preached, as well as unto them: but the word preached did not profit them, not being mixed with faith in them that heard it.
>
> Hebrews 4:1-2

Complete acceptance is to be consistent regarding every promise and at all times. Israel lacked such consistency. They wavered from day-to-day and from promise-to-promise. It cost most of them the promised land, and it cost the younger forty years of their productive lives.

Acceptance of Truth

Faith is not our escape from life's tragedies. Nor is faith gullibility to every get rich scheme, as many televangelists advocate. "Send me one thousand dollars by faith, and God will double your money" is generally a scheme, not a part of the work of faith. They call it "seed money." Why do the "faith preachers" not plant their own "seed money" instead of using yours? Because their ministry is generally not about you being blessed; it's about them paying their exorbitant program expenses—and some have been proven to live extravagant lives of luxury. This is not to say that we should not give to legitimate causes, and I am not suggesting we should not obey the law of tithing and offerings. But I am suggesting we need to participate in that which is truth: not the religious scams.

Contrary to many religious gimmicks, faith is to believe in the truth of the Scripture: God and His promises are truth. Our faith needs to have a reference point in the Word of God. This will keep us from erring in our requests to God, and it will keep us from falling prey to religious scams and unrealistic personal ambitions, which are often grandiose dreams unanchored to God's will and purpose for our lives. I can give you an embarrassing list of my own dreams and prayers, that if accomplished, they may well have left me crushed on the rocks of arrogance. It is sometimes difficult to decipher between God's will and personal ambition. Every small voice in our lives is not the voice of God; it's sometimes a conglomerate of sincerity, naivety, gullibility, pride, and absurdity. Anything apart from God's Word may be challenged as to whether or not it is truth. "Jesus saith unto him, I am the way, the truth, and the life: no man cometh unto the Father, but by me" (John 14:6). "Sanctify them through thy truth: thy word is truth" (John 17:17). Our faith must be predicated upon God's Word.

James warned that we are not to make requests that dishonor God by being contrary to His Word. "Ye ask, and receive not, because ye ask amiss, that ye may consume it upon your lusts" (James 4:3). Still, when we ask in faith those things which are pleasing to God, we can expect to receive them. "Verily, verily, I say unto you, He that believeth on me, the works that I do shall he do also; and greater works than these shall he do; because I go unto my Father. And whatsoever ye shall ask in my name, that will I do, that the Father may be glorified in the Son. If ye shall ask any thing in my name, I will do it" (John 14:12-14).

Truth That Cannot Be Proven

Our faith is in a God we cannot see, although we see evidence of His presence, and we experience His presence within our lives—though this spiritual experience needs to harmonize with the directives of Scripture. We believe in the God of a book—the Bible—of which no known original copy exists: the oldest partial text of Old Testament Scripture dates to around the second century B.C.. and the oldest known complete copy of Old Testament Scripture is about 1000 years old. Though we cannot physically prove the authenticity of the Bible, our faith in the Bible as the inspired Word of God brings results based upon the Bible, and these results strengthen our trust in God and His Word.

We all begin with what the Bible terms "a measure of faith," which grows as we exercise that measure of faith. "For I say, through the grace given unto me, to every man that is among you, not to think of himself more highly than he ought to think; but to think soberly, according as God hath dealt to every man the measure of faith" (Romans 12:3). If we fail to act upon this innate faith, we are susceptible to fear, doubt, cynicism, and the deception of Satan. In his letter to the Roman church, Paul describes the downward spiral from faith to decadence.

> For I am not ashamed of the gospel of Christ: for it is the power of God unto salvation to every one that believeth; to the Jew first, and also to the Greek. For therein is the righteousness of God revealed from faith to faith: as it is written, The just shall live by faith. For the wrath of God is revealed from heaven against all ungodliness and unrighteousness of men, who hold the truth in unrighteousness; Because that which may be known of God is manifest in them; for God hath shewed it unto them. For the invisible things of him from the creation of the world are clearly seen, being understood by the things that are made, even his eternal power and Godhead; so that they are without excuse: Because that, when they knew God, they glorified him not as God, neither were thankful; but became vain in their imaginations, and their foolish heart was darkened. Professing themselves to be wise, they became fools, And changed the glory of the uncorruptible God into an image made like to corruptible man, and to birds, and fourfooted beasts, and creeping things. Wherefore God also gave them up to uncleanness through the lusts of their own hearts, to dishonour their own bodies between themselves: Who changed the truth of God into a lie, and worshipped and served the creature more than the Creator, who is blessed for ever. Amen.

> Romans 1:16-25

Man is not arbitrarily selected for salvation; conversely, built into every individual, every generation, and every culture is a connection to God. We strengthen that link by acting upon the God given faith; contrariwise, when we reject God's extended hand of grace, we gravitate to the baseness of our fallen nature, with the potential for total depravity, void of a conscience toward God.

Consider the scriptural definition of faith: "Now faith is the substance of things hoped for, the evidence of things not seen" (Hebrews11:1). Let's diagnose the key words:

- Faith: the word itself—faith—is intangible. Faith cannot be detected by the senses (we can't taste it, touch it, smell it, see it, nor hear it); however, when we experience faith—when faith gets in our hearts—it becomes tangible. Faith becomes definite, perceivable, and objective in personal experience. Consider that we are unable to see love, but when we experience love there is no doubt as to its existence.

- Substance: the matter, stuff, material of which a thing is made. Therefore, faith is the tangible existence of our hopes: our hopes go from an intangible desire (wish) to a present existence. Hope, without faith, is in the future tense; however, when faith enters, the hope becomes present tense. Faith is the substance of which our hopes are made. Matthew Henry wrote regarding faith: It " . . . is a firm persuasion and expectation that God will perform all that He has promised to us in Christ; and this persuasion is so strong that it gives the soul a kind of possession and present fruition of those things, gives them a subsistence in the soul . . . " [2]

When I was younger, I always hoped to receive certain gifts at Christmas. For weeks and even months I would talk and dream about my hopes. A few days before Christmas, the family raised the Christmas tree, and my parents placed gift-wrapped boxes underneath. The wrapped boxes were the "substance" of my hopes. Could I see the gifts? No, but I believed that inside those boxes were my presents. Because I knew my parents' character, I could be confident the Christmas gift was something I desired.

Our hopes—though intangible—become substance: something

we are sure about. This happens when faith consumes our hearts. We soar into another realm. Our persuasion that we will receive something from God becomes so strong that we count the days left until we get to open our gift. That's why we praise God before the miracle happens. Faith produces praise. In the Old Testament, the Lord rebuked Israel because they lacked this element of faith. They were often praising God on the wrong side of their miracles: after the miracle rather than before.

- Evidence: anything that provides material or information on which a conclusion or proof may be based. Faith is that which provides material or information from which you and I form a conclusion, though we can't visibly see the finished outcome. The gift-wrapped box is the evidence that the gift is present; however, the actual gift is yet unseen by the natural eye. Matthew Henry continues, "Faith demonstrates to the eye of the mind the reality of those things that cannot be discerned by the eye of the body . . . it is designed to serve the believer instead of sight, and to be to the soul all that the senses are to the body."[3] Paul expressed, "For we walk by faith, not by sight" (II Corinthians 5:7). Faith is like trusting the instrument gages in order to fly into the clouds or through the storm.

Faith, however, is not blind trust; rather, it is seeing with a different set of eyes other than the natural. If you can see or prove something with the natural senses, then it is not faith; it is knowledge. Faith is present when something can only be seen through confidence in God and His Word. Faith does not come through book knowledge; rather, it comes through trusting the God of Scripture. Paul expressed the source of faith when he said, "So then faith cometh by hearing, and hearing by the word of God" (Romans 10:17).

For the Christian, faith is different than positive thinking; faith is a spiritual state of mind we arrive at because of our knowledge and trust in God and the Scripture. Faith is a state of complete trust in the God of Scripture: believing anything is possible with God. "But Jesus beheld them, and said unto them, With men this is impossible; but with God all things are possible" (Matthew 19:26). Faith is a spiritual state in between your needs and the reality of receiving an answer from God. Faith is the first step toward our miracle. We don't usually go from a need to a miracle; rather, we go from a need, to faith, to a miracle. It is in this spiritual state of faith that the need is as good as met; for in this state we are in total confidence of God's ability, love, and wisdom; therefore, if our request is in God's will, it shall be done if we remain in a state of faith. Any part of our Christian walk that lacks faith renders us a disappointment to God. "But without faith it is impossible to please Him . . . " (Hebrews 11:6). A carpenter needs a hammer and saw. An artist needs paint, brushes, and a canvas. A surgeon needs steady hands and good vision. A Christian needs faith in God.

Chapter 8

SAVING FAITH

We must not think of faith only in terms of a miracle of healing or provision. These, though significant, have to do with the physical man; therefore, they are temporal. The most important aspect of faith is the role it plays in bringing us salvation and in living a Christian life. These have to do with the spiritual man; therefore, they are eternal. Faith is the key component of salvation; it is impossible to be saved without faith. Even God's awesome grace does not save us unless appropriated by a personal response of faith.

Salvation is by the grace of God. God conceived, brought about, and presented the plan of salvation to man for his personal acceptance or rejection. God's grace doesn't originate from our merit: it is the gift of God. We were spiritually dead, but God offered us new spiritual life. We were servants of Satan and sin. God offered us deliverance from both. Our sin had separated us from God's fellowship; nonetheless, God invited us back into His family. We were under the curse of eternal damnation; still, God offered to reverse the curse and to give us eternal life. All of the above benefits, man could not accomplish of himself. No amount of personal effort could accomplish even one of these; yet, God made them available by His grace. Further, salvation came about not because man pleaded to

God for redemption; rather, God's love for His creation motivated Him to reach for us. The prophet Isaiah's description of God's plea says it best: "Come now, and let us reason together, saith the Lord: though your sins be as scarlet, they shall be as white as snow; though they be red like crimson, they shall be as wool" (Isaiah 1:18).

This is where faith enters the picture. God places grace on the table for our consideration, but we have to accept the deal. This marvelous grace of God is initiated in our lives by our personal faith in God. "For by grace are ye saved through faith; and that not of yourselves: it is the gift of God: not of works, lest any man should boast" (Ephesians 2:8-9). Faith in Jesus Christ is essential for salvation; otherwise, the grace of God could be appropriated into the life of those who do not want it—Hitler and Stalin and Saddam Hussein would be saved if grace were a blanket covering. Does this not suggest that man is somewhat earning salvation by the act of believing? No. God placed within every human an element of faith to enact the gift of grace. God's grace is a gift. The faith to appropriate grace is also a gift from God. This graciousness of our Creator makes salvation totally unearned by man; instead, it is God's gift to man. We activate faith in our hearts by our own will; likewise, we can destroy the faith God has given us by our choosing to do so.

I previously stated that within each of our lives is a "measure of faith" (Romans 12:3), and it is enough to allow us, once we hear the Gospel message, to believe in Jesus Christ. This belief in Jesus Christ starts the personal process of salvation. Saving faith is that singular moment that brings grace into our lives; moreover, it is the beginning of an attitude that continues with us throughout life, allowing us to " . . . grow in grace, and in the knowledge of our Lord and Savior Jesus Christ" (II Peter 3:18). Our faith in Jesus Christ must continue, else, in this spiritual journey, we drift from the way, or even return to our former carnal ways.

There exists, however, both a saving faith (of which we have been reading) and what has been termed acknowledging faith (verbally proclaiming our belief in God but not necessarily acting upon it for salvation). To believe that God exists is acknowledging faith, which many misrepresent as being sufficient for salvation. Let me explain. We can all agree that Satan is not saved; yet, Satan believes in God. "Thou believest that there is one God; thou doest well: the devils also believe, and tremble" (James 2:19). Satan has faith that God exists: Satan knows that God exists, for he has even experienced God as his creator and—not meaning to be lighthearted—as his boss. The prophet Ezekiel of the Old Testament had keen spiritual insight regarding the spiritual forces at work against God. He prophesied regarding the Prince of Tyrus in a manner some commentators think was a veiled reference to Satan: "Thou art the anointed cherub that covereth; and I have set thee so: thou wast upon the holy mountain of God; thou hast walked up and down in the midst of the stones of fire. Thou wast perfect in thy ways from the day that thou wast created, till iniquity was found in thee" (Ezekiel 28:14-15). Satan, who has fought long and hard against God, has no question as to the existence of God. Still, Satan's acknowledgement of God's existence does not save him; on the contrary, it condemns him. Satan's acknowledgment of God's existence has similarities to "acknowledging faith," the primary difference being that Satan has seen God, and so his acknowledgment is more than faith. Acknowledging faith in its raw form is simply to acknowledge or affirm that we believe in God, that is, that we believe God exists, and even that He saves the lost. Such acknowledgement of God does not appropriate grace, for it does not actively seek God. Acknowledgement of God does not prompt obedience or cause one to bear the fruit of the Spirit. Acknowledging faith does not, within itself, draw us near to God; rather, we simply acknowledge that we believe in God. The manner in which some people are mass introduced to Christ is somewhat disconcerting, for it seems the introduction is more akin to acknowledging faith rather than saving faith. Saving faith has an extended effect, like: "And when Jesus came to the place, he looked up, and saw him, and said unto him, Zacchaeus, make haste, and come down; for to day I must abide at thy house" (Luke 19:5), or like: "And they continued stedfastly in the apostles' doctrine and fellowship, and in breaking of bread, and in prayers" (Acts 2:42).

Saving faith is different than acknowledging faith in that saving faith causes us to respond in a positive way toward God: moving toward God. Saving faith is an active faith—there is no example in Scripture of a saved person responding passively. Though we can't earn the grace of God, because of our faith, we act upon the grace of God extended to us. Faith causes us to reach out our hand to the extended hand of God's grace. This faith exceeds an acknowledging about God, or even a profession of faith in Christ; instead, saving faith causes us to respond to the God in whom we believe. We always leave differently than we came.

Saving faith is evidenced by a submission of Lordship to Jesus Christ and a turning—from sin and Satan—to God and righteousness. This process generally begins with repentance, which is the first step in the New Birth experience, and the process continues as we grow in the grace of Christ. From personal experience, my first act of saving faith was at a revival service when I was about thirteen years old. My response that night at the revival service was to "walk the isle" and recite a sinners prayer. I can't remember the type church, or the evangelist, and I never returned. Sadly, no one shared with me the steps of the New Birth. But I did act upon my faith. And I believe God acknowledged my faith, for during the next couple years I continued to pray, acknowledge my need of Christ, and periodically attend church. Finally, I was introduced to the Bible, greater truth, and the necessity of the New Birth experience. At each step in my experience, I acted upon faith: this is what I mean by saving faith.

Why do we include the New Birth as essential for salvation? The New Birth experience replicates the death, burial, and resurrection of Christ. The experience includes repentance (a turning from sin and to God), water baptism into Christ (appropriating His death to our sins), and the infilling of the Holy Spirit (the resurrection power of Christ resides within us). Once we have completed this experience of salvation, we develop a love for God's Word and a tremendous desire to live a transformed life of continual love for, and devotion to, Jesus Christ. New Testament saving faith is never passive; rather, it is acting out our faith instead of talking about faith. Saving faith prompts us, like the believers in the first century church, to submit to baptism in the name of the Lord Jesus Christ (Mark 16:16; Acts 2:38, 8:12, 14-16; 9:17-18; 10:44-48; 16:15, 33; 19:1-6). Saving faith allows us, like the first believers of Christ, to receive the baptism of the Holy Spirit (Matthew 3:11; John 7:38-39; Acts 2:1-4; 10:44-47; 19:6). Saving faith does not stop at the confession of sins; it becomes a life long companion, motivating and directing our lives.

Saving faith and obedience to God's Word grow together inseparably. The "measure of faith" in our hearts (mentioned earlier) is activated by obedience to Jesus Christ. The measure of faith given to each of us is sufficient for us to appropriate God's grace in our lives. Though we have this measure of faith, we have a will (a God given right to decide), and we can choose to believe or disbelieve God's Word, to follow or reject Christ. Rejection of Christ dulls our measure of faith, and can ultimately lead to a total loss of faith. That is why many live as if they have no sensitivity toward God. The ultimate travesty is for God to give us over to a "reprobate mind," unable to believe in God. Consequently, once we reach such a state, we cannot appropriate the grace of God apart from another miracle of God's grace—the prayers of a mother or grandmother (or some such act) may cause God to restore His grace to us.

To say that faith is the only requirement for salvation is misleading at best and deceptive at worst. Scriptures that link faith and salvation as one and the same are often misinterpreted, are at best incomplete, and often overlook the insurmountable evidence of Scriptures that describe saving faith as "faith in action." Our faith must go beyond acknowledging that we believe in God. We must enter into a saving faith relationship: faith that causes us to respond to God according to His Word.

Is saving faith so elusive that we go through life with our fingers crossed, hoping we are saved? Can we know we have saving faith, or is such simply a game of wait and see? No, we don't have to second-guess our salvation experience. There are conditions for saving faith recorded in the Holy Scripture. Jesus challenged, "Search the scriptures; for in them ye think ye have eternal life: and they are they which testify of me" (John 5:39). The Jewish religious leaders had their own set of guidelines, some biblical and others manmade. Jesus proclaimed, "Search the scriptures," for the Bible is God's guideline for saving faith. Consider what the Bible says about saving faith and accept God's Word as the sole rule of faith.

First, saving faith leads us to the New Birth experience (as before mentioned). To be born again, we must have died—not physically—spiritually. In contrast to the old man, controlled by the carnal spirit, the born again man is under the control of God's Spirit. Once we have experienced the New Birth, as we continue to live in this realm of saving faith, our lives take on certain features that are the results of saving faith. Jesus expressed, "By this shall all men know that ye are my disciples, if ye have love one to another" (John 13:35).

Loving one another is not earning salvation, for salvation is the gift of God, but it is the evidence of saving faith at work in our lives and that we are growing in the grace of God. Saving faith, as defined by Scripture, is more than words: it is based upon the truth of God's Word, thus it is obedience to God's Word. Jesus commanded, "If ye love me, keep my commandments" (John 14:15).

Second, saving faith is more than a feeling. Saving faith causes us to change our lifestyles from the works of the flesh to the works of the Holy Spirit (people will notice a change of the fruit we bear), thus, saving faith is faith in action. In explaining the New Birth to the devout religious ruler Nicodemus (John 3), Jesus used the analogy of wind. Saving faith, like the presence of wind, though perceived as invisible, will produce signs of its presence. Saving faith is more than a thought about God; rather, it is an attitude that links us to the purpose of God. Such faith is a heart response; we express how we inwardly feel about Christ not by words alone but by a personal devotion and loyalty to Him, which is evident by the life we live. It is one thing to say we have saving faith, it is another thing to live a life that is the result of saving faith active within our hearts. The Apostle Paul wrote: "Examine yourselves, whether ye be in the faith; prove your own selves . . . " (II Corinthians 13:5). It becomes our responsibility to continually appraise our faith, to see if it is in harmony with the scriptural definition of saving faith, recognizing that we can be detoured by the adversary. Further, faith can be lost. To loose our faith leads us to live apart from the grace of God; consequently, without grace we will fail God miserably. "Looking diligently lest any man fail of the grace of God; lest any root of bitterness springing up trouble you, and thereby many be defiled" (Hebrews 12:15). The Apostle Peter, who knew well the emotion of failing Christ, warned us: "For if after they have escaped the pollutions of the world through the knowledge of the Lord and Saviour Jesus Christ, they are again entangled therein, and overcome, the latter end is worse with them than the beginning. For it had been better for them not to have known the way of righteousness, than, after they have known it, to turn from the holy commandment delivered unto them" (II Peter 2:20-21).

Finally, the grace of God should remain daily active in our lives until Jesus calls us home. We must continue on and finish the journey of grace. Paul's writings to the churches encouraged continuation in saving faith. "And you, that were sometime alienated and enemies in your mind by wicked works, yet now hath he reconciled in the body of his flesh through death, to present you holy and unblameable and unreproveable in his sight: If ye continue in the faith grounded and settled, and be not moved away from the hope of the gospel . . . " (Colossians 1:21-23).

Likewise, James the half-brother of Christ, who rose to leadership in the Jerusalem church, not only warned against passive religion, but he offered directives on duties Christians should observe:

> But whoso looketh into the perfect law of liberty, and continueth therein, he being not a forgetful hearer, but a doer of the work, this man shall be blessed in his deed. If any man among you seem to be religious, and bridleth not his tongue, but deceiveth his own heart, this man's religion is vain. Pure religion and undefiled before God and the Father is this, To visit the fatherless and widows in their affliction, and to keep himself unspotted from the world.
>
> James 1:25-27

Paul used several terms (to describe the Christian walk) that constitute action: fight, warfare, and wrestle. He even likened the Christian life to a race, mentioning two qualities that encapsulate a successful race: run as fast as you can and finish. There is no place for passivity in a race. Further, it is God's grace that enables us in the Christian race. "And he said unto me, My grace is sufficient for thee: for my strength is made perfect in weakness. Most gladly therefore will I rather glory in my infirmities, that the power of Christ may rest upon me" (II Corinthians 12:9). If we drop out of the race, it is not because God's grace is insufficient; rather, our failure lies within our refusal to maintain an attitude of saving faith. Somewhere along the way we choose not to walk in saving faith: obedience to Christ's Word, a changed lifestyle, actively seeking after the Holy Spirit's will, an attitude of personal devotion, and loyalty to Christ. Sometimes we drift back into an acknowledging faith, thus the absence of saving faith conforms us to this world and all its ways; in contrast, saving faith transforms us into a life well pleasing unto Jesus Christ. Paul pleaded with the Roman Christians to engage in saving faith when he wrote to them:

> I beseech you therefore, brethren, by the mercies of God, that ye present your bodies a living sacrifice, holy, acceptable unto God, which is your reasonable service. And be not conformed to this world: but be ye transformed by the renewing of your mind, that ye may prove what is that good, and acceptable, and perfect, will of God. For I say, through the grace given unto me, to every man that is among you, not to think of himself more highly than he ought to think; but to think soberly, according as God hath dealt to every man the measure of faith.

> Romans 12:1-3

In reiteration, three qualities constitute saving faith: experiencing the New Birth, maintaining an active Christian lifestyle, and continuing in such until Christ calls us home by way of death or the rapture. Anything less tends to be mere acknowledging faith: something the devil does well.

Chapter 9

EVIDENCE OF SAVING FAITH

True faith—saving faith—produces visible manifestations of the inward working of faith. I prefer the term "saving faith" in lieu of faith, for the carnal man may have faith in something—his ability, his associations, his wealth—apart from God. Our day-to-day lifestyles reveal saving faith or a lack of faith in our hearts. Still, an overabundance of good works doesn't necessarily constitute faith—faithless people can be highly motivated toward good deeds apart from serving God. The millions of dollars given away annually by agnostics and atheists to philanthropic causes is proof positive. Good deeds motivated by saving faith never have a personal agenda, and they will always promote Christ, not the individual. Conversely, a life of good deeds, apart from faith, is considered by Scripture to be "dead works." A God centered faith is necessary to produce godly results—righteousness. We have Abraham as our example:

> [But] if so, what shall we say about Abraham, our forefather humanly speaking—[what did he] find out? [How does this affect his position, and what was gained by him?] For if Abraham was justified (estab-

lished as just by acquittal from guilt) by good works [that he did, then] he has grounds for boasting. But not before God! For what does the Scripture say? Abraham believed in (trusted in) God, and it was credited to his account as righteousness (right living and right standing with God).

Romans 4:1-3 AMP

Abraham's righteousness did not come through the covenant act of circumcision; rather, it came when he believed God's promises—faith. The God of the Old Testament selected Abraham, originally called Abram, to perpetuate the message of monotheism. He called him to leave the city of Ur. The settlement of Ur was as old as known history: settled sometime around 4000 B.C. The area began as a farming community, and because of its location along the Euphrates River near the Persian Gulf, it became a city of culture, commerce, and wealth. Because of its year-round farming and ability to store food, Ur became the principle city of the region, and by the time of Abraham it was the world's largest city, numbering sixty-five thousand inhabitants.

A series of kings ruled this city of highly advanced infrastructure and government. It had a written language that recorded its laws and religion. In time, Ur became the capital of the earliest known empire, the Sumerian Empire, which lasted some three thousand years, until surpassed by the Babylonian Empire. The area of this biblical city along the Euphrates River, about one hundred miles southeast of the ancient city of Babylon, is known today as Iraq. God called Abraham to leave this land behind and travel to a land He would reveal. The call of God came to Abram at a time when idolatry was the norm among the people of the Mesopotamian Valley. It was a two-fold call: a call for separation from his present habitat, rife with idolatry and evil; a call for separation unto the one true God of heaven to accomplish His purpose.

Faith in God motivated Abram to obedience: leave and follow. Abram's obedience to God's call eventually removed him from the polytheistic culture of his ancestors. The moon god, Sin, was the guardian deity of the city of Abram's birth. This deity was also the head of the pantheon dominating the Euphrates Valley. Abram left Ur, his destination uncertain, for God led him without revealing prearranged instructions, but his purpose was crystal clean: preserve monotheism. It is no marvel that God called Abram to separate himself from the idolatrous practices, which dominated the lives of the valley inhabitants. In revealing Himself to Abram as the one true God, it was as if God started His creation over, with a single family, in a land far removed from their birth. Before God fulfilled His promise to Abram (his descendants would be a great nation), Abram had to first believe God. He eventually passed the test, and God changed his name from Abram (exalted father) to Abraham (father of a multitude). The promise could now come.

Though his wife Sarah was beyond the age of childbearing, he believed God's promise to produce a nation from their descendants. "And being not weak in faith, he considered not his own body now dead, when he was about an hundred years old, neither yet the deadness of Sarah's womb" (Romans 4:19). The answer to the promise came in a son of their old age, Isaac. Because Abraham believed God would fulfill His promise, he was willing to obey the strange demand from God to offer as a sacrifice his son Isaac: his only know means of the promise being fulfilled. This test was necessary for Abraham to arise to the heights in God that he did, for a life that boasts of faith, but produces no faithful attributes, is considered "dead faith." Abraham's example to us is one of life: not death. The New Testament writer James used Abraham's life to express the ineptness of "dead faith."

> But wilt thou know, O vain man, that faith without works is dead? Was not Abraham our father justified by works, when he had offered Isaac his son upon the altar? Seest thou how faith wrought with his works, and by works was faith made perfect? And the scripture was fulfilled which saith, Abraham believed God, and it was imputed unto him for righteousness: and he was called the Friend of God. Ye see then how that by works a man is justified, and not by faith only.

> James 3:20-24

Faith without good works is "dead faith." Good works without faith is "dead works." Neither is pleasing to Christ. As the natural life is structured with "cause and effect" design, so is the spiritual life. The cause (faith) has an effect (Christian works of righteousness). With this in mind, it is good for us to examine our profession of faith. One of the best possible scenarios in which to examine our faith is in the midst of a crisis. How do I respond when disaster strikes? Do I fall apart? Do I look for someone to blame? Do I feel hurt at God? Do I go on a personal guilt trip condemning myself? Do I go into attack mode, shouting and accusing everyone around me? Do I resort to staying home from church and avoiding personal devotions? Do I resort to overeating, or abusing my body with drugs, alcohol, or cigarettes? All of these are indications that I do not truly possess saving faith. I may profess, but I do not possess, for if saving faith controls my life, I will respond positively toward God and the Bible.

Our lack of faith has adverse results: fear, doubt, negativism, and insecurity. Without faith, these all dominate our personal lives; further, we become poor role models for those who look to us for an example of spirituality. Operating by faith takes away personal control and leaves God as captain of our ship; we are no longer " . . . the master of my fate: . . . the captain of my soul."[1] God is in charge. When the storms of disaster set in, faith causes us to respond positively in spite of the surrounding circumstances: we hoist the sails, or look for the rainbow, or search the horizon for a glimpse of the Lord walking our way on the water. Though our spirits may be intense with excitement (for it is true, "part of the fun is the battle itself"), the soul is at peace, knowing that Christ is the master of any and all storms; conversely, when we lack faith, and the storms of disaster set in, we are tempted to reef the sails for fear of capsizing, or lower the lifeboats and abandon the ship altogether. Our souls are in turmoil, often fearing the worst possible outcome. Our energy is consumed by worry, and we do not feel up to working through the problem. We readily see that a lack of faith brings a sense of personal despair and ultimately defeat.

Not only does our lack of faith bring personal defeat, it also sends an improper message to those we model. In his book, *Living Out The Book of Acts*, Bruce Larson, in a chapter he entitles *Picnics in the Storm*, paints this picture quite well. He explains:

> We learn our behaviors and attitudes from models. Psychologists for example, are discovering that some types of animal behavior are not innate at all. Monkeys taken from their mothers at a very young age, having had no experience of being mothered, don't know what to do with their own young. Mothering apparently is a learned skill. All of us learn behavior patterns from the primary people in our lives who provide us with models."[2]

Perhaps this is a clue to why alcoholic parents often produce children that become alcoholics. Could it be that the danger toward alcoholism is not in the genes; rather, it is in the guidance—or lack thereof—of the parents? Though some individuals seem more susceptible to addiction, I believe the real problem lies in the modeling of parents. Furthermore, this is a partial answer to why adults who were abused as children abuse their own children, and a clue to why a young woman whose father abused her mother, marries a man who abuses her. The cycle too often continues. Likewise, our professing of faith, yet our negative response in the face of adversity, are poor examples which others may model. This is why faith in God and Scripture needs to dominate our lives.

Our lives either bring a calming effect in the midst of life's storms, or we send a message of alarm and oftentimes despair. We should read again the account of the twelve spies sent by Moses to search out the land of promise (Numbers 13). The twelve spies expressed their faith: "And they told him, and said, We came unto the land whither thou sentest us, and surely it floweth with milk and honey; and this is the fruit of it" (Numbers 13:27). The emphasis of faith is in the word "surely." If only they had stopped there and clung to that thought, but their report didn't stop with an expression of faith. Except for Joshua and Caleb, the report digressed into the realm of doubt, then disbelief that they could possess the Promised Land. "Nevertheless the people be strong that dwell in the land, and the cities are walled, and very great: and moreover we saw the children of Anak there" (Numbers 13:28). Two words, "nevertheless" and "moreover," rendered the promises of God invalid. The faithless reports of ten sent a negative response throughout the camp of Israel. The people panicked. Their response cost them forty years, minus the two they had already spent, wandering in the wilderness. We are either stress reducers or stress producers, faith builders or faith wreckers.

Take a look at the Apostle Paul's response to a storm at sea. Consider the situation as Luke recorded it:

> And when the south wind blew softly, supposing that they had obtained their purpose, loosing thence, they sailed close by Crete. But not long after there arose against it a tempestuous wind, called Euroclydon. And when the ship was caught, and could not bear up into the wind, we let her drive. And running under a certain island which is called Clauda, we had much work to come by the boat: Which when they had taken up, they used helps, undergirding the ship; and, fearing lest they should fall into the quicksands, strake sail, and so were driven. And we being exceedingly tossed with a tempest, the next day they lightened the ship; And the third day we cast out with our own hands the tackling of the ship. And when neither sun nor stars in many days appeared, and no small tempest lay on us, all hope that we should be saved was then taken away. But after long abstinence Paul stood forth in the midst of them, and said, Sirs, ye should have hearkened unto me, and not have loosed from Crete, and to have gained this harm and loss. And now I exhort you to be of good cheer: for there shall be no loss of any man's life among you, but of the ship. For there stood by me this night the angel of God, whose I am, and whom I serve, Saying, Fear not, Paul; thou must be brought before Caesar: and, lo, God hath given thee all them that sail with thee. Wherefore, sirs, be of good cheer: for I believe

God, that it shall be even as it was told me. Howbeit we must be cast upon a certain island. But when the fourteenth night was come, as we were driven up and down in Adria, about midnight the shipmen deemed that they drew near to some country; And sounded, and found it twenty fathoms: and when they had gone a little further, they sounded again, and found it fifteen fathoms. Then fearing lest we should have fallen upon rocks, they cast four anchors out of the stern, and wished for the day. And as the shipmen were about to flee out of the ship, when they had let down the boat into the sea, under colour as though they would have cast anchors out of the foreship, Paul said to the centurion and to the soldiers, Except these abide in the ship, ye cannot be saved. Then the soldiers cut off the ropes of the boat, and let her fall off. And while the day was coming on, Paul besought them all to take meat, saying, This day is the fourteenth day that ye have tarried and continued fasting, having taken nothing. Wherefore I pray you to take some meat: for this is for your health: for there shall not an hair fall from the head of any of you. And when he had thus spoken, he took bread, and gave thanks to God in presence of them all: and when he had broken it, he began to eat. Then were they all of good cheer, and they also took some meat.

Acts 27:13-36

While others were clinging to the thread of desperation, Paul manifests a calming attitude. Paul suggests, "Since God is in charge, and this storm will pass, and we will make it, let's eat dinner."

Larson writes regarding these Scriptures: "This kind of witness in the midst of disaster is what authentic faith is all about."[3] Larson ccontinues, " . . . Handling disasters, large or small, is a test of our faith. We are modeling for others our fear or faith, our panic or confidence. When disasters hit, don't waste them. Be the one who says, "Let's have a picnic."[4]

What are some of the evidences of faith in our life? Bernard Koerselman, in his work, *What The Bible Says About Saving Faith*, explains, "James said that our faith—if it is a saving faith— must be visible. I see three visible signs of a saving faith—obedience, fruit, and good works— three different perspectives by which anyone can tell there is something different and special about us because of our faith."[5]

I've heard speakers give inspiring sermons on the grace of God, sharing Scriptures that, if one was not familiar with an overall concept of the Bible, would accept the teaching of passivity in salvation: by this I mean God does everything and we do nothing. I've heard the Christian journey described as taking an airplane ride where the ticket is free, and all you have to do is get on board and enjoy the ride. Yet, a study of Scripture reveals that the Christian walk is one of an uphill journey, fighting Satan and sin, and striving to please our Lord in the face of much opposition. This effort is not to earn salvation, but much personal effort is possible because of the saving grace of God that has come to us. Salvation makes us acceptable in Christ's sight, but it also enlists us into the army of the Lord. Anything less than this could well be a sign that one has not experienced saving faith, and consequently has not experienced salvation, for salvation is " . . . by grace through faith . . . " (Ephesians 2:8), and faith is seldom, if ever, passive, for faith produces personal action. Even when faith seems passive, it is taking great effort on the part of the believer to remain in that passive state—actively passive. Though grace cannot be earned, God's grace is activated by our faith, which takes effort on our part, and saving faith leaves evidence of its presence. Faith is our access into the grace of God. "By whom also we have access by faith into this grace wherein we stand, and rejoice in hope of the glory of God" (Romans 5:2).

Since grace is not appropriated in an individual life apart from saving faith, and faith leaves evidence of its presence, we who are saved should show forth evidence of our salvation by a changed lifestyle. Consider Scriptures that express a visibly changed life as evidence of faith and grace.

Faith activates saving grace

> And he said to the woman, Thy faith hath saved thee;
> go in peace.
>
> Luke 7:50

> By whom also we have access by faith into this grace
> wherein we stand, and rejoice in hope of the glory of
> God.
>
> Romans 5:2

> For unto us was the gospel preached, as well as unto
> them: but the word preached did not profit them, not
> being mixed with faith in them that heard it.
>
> Hebrews 4:2

Faith brings us to repentance (a turning from sin)

> To open their eyes, and to turn them from darkness
> to light, and from the power of Satan unto God, that
> they may receive forgiveness of sins, and inheritance
> among them which are sanctified by faith that is in
> me.
>
> Acts 26:18

> Now I rejoice, not that ye were made sorry, but that ye
> sorrowed to repentance: for ye were made sorry after
> a godly manner, that ye might receive damage by us
> in nothing. For godly sorrow worketh repentance to
> salvation not to be repented of: but the sorrow of the
> world worketh death.
>
> II Corinthians 7:9-10

Faith brings us into the New Birth experience

He that believeth and is baptized shall be saved; but he that believeth not shall be damned.

Mark 16:16

And brought them out, and said, Sirs, what must I do to be saved? And they said, Believe on the Lord Jesus Christ, and thou shalt be saved, and thy house. And they spake unto him the word of the Lord, and to all that were in his house. And he took them the same hour of the night, and washed their stripes; and was baptized, he and all his, straightway.

Acts 16:30-33

This only would I learn of you, Received ye the Spirit by the works of the law, or by the hearing of faith? That the blessing of Abraham might come on the Gentiles through Jesus Christ; that we might receive the promise of the Spirit through faith.

Galatians 3:2, 14

Faith produces obedience to God according to His Word

But now is made manifest, and by the scriptures of the prophets, according to the commandment of the everlasting God, made known to all nations for the obedience of faith.

Romans 16:26

Be ye therefore followers of God, as dear children;

114

And walk in love, as Christ also hath loved us, and hath given himself for us an offering and a sacrifice to God for a sweetsmelling savour. But fornication, and all uncleanness, or covetousness, let it not be once named among you, as becometh saints; Neither filthiness, nor foolish talking, nor jesting, which are not convenient: but rather giving of thanks. For this ye know, that no whoremonger, nor unclean person, nor covetous man, who is an idolater, hath any inheritance in the kingdom of Christ and of God. Let no man deceive you with vain words: for because of these things cometh the wrath of God upon the children of disobedience. Be not ye therefore partakers with them.

Ephesians 5:1-7

Wherefore lay apart all filthiness and superfluity of naughtiness, and receive with meekness the engrafted word, which is able to save your souls. But be ye doers of the word, and not hearers only, deceiving your own selves. For if any be a hearer of the word, and not a doer, he is like unto a man beholding his natural face in a glass: For he beholdeth himself, and goeth his way, and straightway forgetteth what manner of man he was. But whoso looketh into the perfect law of liberty, and continueth therein, he being not a forgetful hearer, but a doer of the work, this man shall be blessed in his deed.

James 1:21-25

Faith produces righteous living through the Spirit walk

For we through the Spirit wait for the hope of righteousness by faith. This I say then, Walk in the Spirit, and ye shall not fulfil the lust of the flesh. For the flesh lusteth against the Spirit, and the Spirit against

115

the flesh: and these are contrary the one to the other: so that ye cannot do the things that ye would. But if ye be led of the Spirit, ye are not under the law. But the fruit of the Spirit is love, joy, peace, longsuffering, gentleness, goodness, faith, Meekness, temperance: against such there is no law. And they that are Christ's have crucified the flesh with the affections and lusts. If we live in the Spirit, let us also walk in the Spirit. Let us not be desirous of vain glory, provoking one another, envying one another.

Galatians 5:5, 16-18, 22-26

That Christ may dwell in your hearts by faith; that ye, being rooted and grounded in love, May be able to comprehend with all saints what is the breadth, and length, and depth, and height; And to know the love of Christ, which passeth knowledge, that ye might be filled with all the fulness of God.

Ephesians 3:17-19

This I say therefore, and testify in the Lord, that ye henceforth walk not as other Gentiles walk, in the vanity of their mind, Having the understanding darkened, being alienated from the life of God through the ignorance that is in them, because of the blindness of their heart: Who being past feeling have given themselves over unto lasciviousness, to work all uncleanness with greediness. But ye have not so learned Christ; If so be that ye have heard him, and have been taught by him, as the truth is in Jesus: That ye put off concerning the former conversation the old man, which is corrupt according to the deceitful lusts; And be renewed in the spirit of your mind; And that ye put on the new man, which after God is created in righteousness and true holiness. Wherefore putting away lying, speak every man truth with his neighbour: for we are members one of another. Be ye angry, and sin not: let not the sun go down upon your wrath: Neither give place to the devil. Let him that stole steal no more: but rather let him labour, working with his hands the thing which is good, that he may have to give to him that needeth. Let no corrupt communication proceed out of your mouth, but that which is good to the use of edifying, that it may minister grace unto the hearers. And grieve not the holy Spirit of God, whereby ye are sealed unto the day of redemption. Let all bitterness, and wrath, and anger, and clamour, and evil speaking, be put away from you, with all malice: And be ye kind one to another, tenderhearted, forgiving one another, even as God for Christ's sake hath forgiven you.

Ephesians 4:17-32

Faith activates the grace of God in our lives for the miraculous

And, behold, they brought to him a man sick of the palsy, lying on a bed: and Jesus seeing their faith said unto the sick of the palsy; Son, be of good cheer; thy sins be forgiven thee . . . But Jesus turned him about, and when he saw her, he said, Daughter, be of good comfort; thy faith hath made thee whole. And the woman was made whole from that hour.

Matthew 9:2, 22

And his name through faith in his name hath made this man strong, whom ye see and know: yea, the faith which is by him hath given him this perfect soundness in the presence of you all.

Acts 3:16

Faith produces good works (This will be covered in part III)

> What doth it profit, my brethren, though a man say
> he hath faith, and have not works? can faith save
> him? If a brother or sister be naked, and destitute of
> daily food, And one of you say unto them, Depart in
> peace, be ye warmed and filled; notwithstanding ye
> give them not those things which are needful to the
> body; what doth it profit?

> James 2:14-16

Faith produces an active lifestyle of following after God instead of the world

> I beseech you therefore, brethren, by the mercies of
> God, that ye present your bodies a living sacrifice,
> holy, acceptable unto God, which is your reasonable
> service. And be not conformed to this world: but be
> ye transformed by the renewing of your mind, that
> ye may prove what is that good, and acceptable, and
> perfect, will of God. For I say, through the grace giv-
> en unto me, to every man that is among you, not to
> think of himself more highly than he ought to think;
> but to think soberly, according as God hath dealt to
> every man the measure of faith.

> Romans 12:1-3

> For whatsoever is born of God overcometh the world:
> and this is the victory that overcometh the world,
> even our faith.

> I John 5:4

> Love not the world, neither the things that are in the
> world. If any man love the world, the love of the Fa-

ther is not in him. For all that is in the world, the lust of the flesh, and the lust of the eyes, and the pride of life, is not of the Father, but is of the world. And the world passeth away, and the lust thereof: but he that doeth the will of God abideth for ever.

I John 2:15-17

Saving faith is much more than acknowledging belief in Christ. The examples of biblical saving faith are scenes depicting characters whose lives took a radically changed approach to Satan, sin, and the world in which they lived. To espouse any other view of salvation is to live dangerously close to, if not entering into, deception, which is the danger zone bordering apostasy. Of course we cannot expect all to "grow in grace and knowledge of our Lord" at the same growth rate, for Jesus expressed in the parable of the sower, that of those who followed Him, each would produce different amounts of fruit, and some who started would completely fail to follow Him (Matthew 13:3-9). Furthermore, Jesus taught that, the good seed (righteous) and the tares (evil) would grow up together but would be separated in the end (Matthew 13:24-30). Nowhere in Scripture, however, is there given an excuse for failing to mature in Christ; moreover, those who profess Christ, yet after ample time fail to produce good fruit, are in danger of judgment (Matthew 3:8-10). John the Baptist, preparing the way for the Savior, demanded that some (particularly the religious leaders) show evidence of genuine repentance before he would baptize them. Further, Christ began His ministry with a message of repentance. Does this sound like the religion Christ introduced called for a frail faith? A casual confession? An effortless experience? A simple solution? A passive conversion? I don't think so! Consider Christ's words:

Then said Jesus unto his disciples, If any man will come after me, let him deny himself, and take up his cross, and follow me. For whosoever will save his life shall lose it: and whosoever will lose his life for my sake shall find it. For what is a man profited, if he shall gain the whole world, and lose his own soul? or what shall a man give in exchange for his soul?

Matthew 16:24-26

Christ called for complete surrender! Total denial! Absolute obedience! Radical separation! Immediate change! Wholehearted commitment! Why? If He is Lord of our lives, then it must be so. Furthermore, we have not considered the enemy of our soul, aggressive in his attempts to reclaim us for himself by discouragement, deception, and temptation. Anything less than wholehearted devotion to Jesus Christ could very well leave us on the spiritual casualty list. The Apostle Peter, not a novice to the deception of Satan (Luke 22:31-34, 54-62), instructed us in resisting the attacks of Satan on our soul.

Be sober, be vigilant; because your adversary the devil, as a roaring lion, walketh about, seeking whom he may devour: Whom resist stedfast in the faith, knowing that the same afflictions are accomplished in your brethren that are in the world. But the God of all grace, who hath called us unto his eternal glory by Christ Jesus, after that ye have suffered a while, make you perfect, stablish, strengthen, settle you. To him be glory and dominion for ever and ever. Amen.

I Peter 5:8-11

Peter further emphasized that our faith was the first of the many building blocks for a victorious Christian life. Beginning with faith in Jesus Christ, we are to endeavor to build upon that faith. The result is a life pleasing unto our Lord. Notice the instruction from the Scripture to "add to your faith," that is to put forth effort to please Christ by the manner in which we live.

According as his divine power hath given unto us all things that pertain unto life and godliness, through the knowledge of him that hath called us to glory and virtue: Whereby are given unto us exceeding great and precious promises: that by these ye might be partakers of the divine nature, having escaped the corruption that is in the world through lust. And beside this, giving all diligence, add to your faith virtue; and to virtue knowledge; And to knowledge temperance; and to temperance patience; and to patience godliness; And to godliness brotherly kindness; and to brotherly kindness charity. For if these things be in you, and abound, they make you that ye shall neither be barren nor unfruitful in the knowledge of our Lord Jesus Christ. But he that lacketh these things is blind, and cannot see afar off, and hath forgotton that he was purged from his old sins. Wherefore the rather, brethren, give diligence to make your calling and election sure: for if ye do these things, ye shall never fall: For so an entrance shall be ministered unto you abundantly into the everlasting kingdom of our Lord and Saviour Jesus   Christ.

II Peter 1:3-11

From these Scriptures we conclude that we are to be actively involved in Christian maturity. Christian growth takes effort beyond a proclamation of faith. The conclusion of these instructions is quite interesting: "If we do these things we shall never fail" (II Peter 1:10). Could we then deduce that if we do not these things we shall fail? Peter explains, because of our diligence we shall be welcomed into the kingdom with honor (verse 11). Could we also reason that because of a lack of diligence—negligence of "so great salvation" (Hebrews 2:3)—some will hardly enter into heaven, or worse still, be denied entrance. Some are quick to argue this sounds like earning salvation through works; conversely, such teaching warns against neglecting salvation through inactiveness. To earn salvation is impossible; to neglect salvation is inconceivable. As the person with an unregenerate heart leaves evidence of such by the unrighteous lifestyle they live, likewise, our neglected faith leaves evidence that something means more to us than Jesus. Further, a dead faith (words without consistent Christian works) leaves a poor witness to the unsaved,

121

and it sends mixed signals to those that are looking to us for an example. What kind of tracks are we leaving? Just as serious, who's following in our footsteps? In what direction are we leading them?

PART III

WORKS

Chapter 10

CAN GOOD WORKS SAVE US

When I speak of works, it is in a general sense, covering anything we do for the sake of Christ, including: our avoidance of sin, our deeds (of charity, of service to others), Christian devotion (prayer, Bible reading, witnessing, church attendance, tithing), our lifestyle (actions, thoughts, words, places we go, things we do), and applying the many Christian disciplines to our daily lives. This chapter's challenge is, "Can good works save us?" Some say no, and therefore conclude works are not necessary, or at best miniscule in importance, and at the worst a nuisance. Others, reluctantly, say yes—generally with a disclaimer, explaining that Calvary is a partner with good works. A few adamantly defend good works as a part of salvation, often trying to clean the fish before they land it. As I understand works, I have already established their importance; still, the Scripture is clear that salvation does not come from good works. Good works are expected from us of the Lord. Good works are a result of our saving relationship in Christ. The Scripture mandates a life of good works. Good works are the fruit of the Holy Spirit resident in the believer. It's unbelievable that a Christian wouldn't desire good works. All these are true, but not one good work saves us from our sins. Consider this parable of Christ to offer direction in balancing grace, faith, and works.

> Two men went up into the temple to pray; the one a Pharisee, and the other a publican. The Pharisee stood and prayed thus with himself, God, I thank thee, that I am not as other men are, extortioners, unjust, adulterers, or even as this publican. I fast twice in the week, I give tithes of all that I possess. And the publican, standing afar off, would not lift up so much as his eyes unto heaven, but smote upon his breast, saying, God be merciful to me a sinner. I tell you, this man went down to his house justified rather than the other: for every one that exalteth himself shall be abased; and he that humbleth himself shall be exalted.
>
> Luke 18:10-14

This parable reveals two potential attitudes of the heart of mankind (pride and humility): the former drives God away, while the latter brings God near. We might note first what the parable is not teaching.

- It does not teach that we should live unrighteously—God despises unrighteousness.
- It does not teach that we should view sin passively, failing to strive to live an overcoming life—being comfortable with sin affronts God's holiness.

The parable was neither justifying sin nor attacking righteous living; rather, the parable demonstrates how we should approach God—with humility. Queen Esther of the Old Testament gave much consideration to her approach to King Ahasuerus—though this is by no means suggesting an earthly king is a good example of God's kingship. Still, as there are expectations in approaching an earthly king, the parable makes a point about approaching, not just royalty, but Deity—there is a right and wrong attitude in approaching God. The right approach to royalty is to obtain an invitation. The Pharisee's attitude seemed more like, "I have a right to be here because of the way I live. I've earned this right by being, doing, obeying, conforming, sacrificing, and more." We must admit this fella did have an impressive religious resume. He was:

- Not an extortionist: he made his living fairly.
- Not unjust: he lived by the golden rule (or so he thought).
- Not an adulterer: he was morally clean.
- Very religious: he fasted twice a week, tithed on all he possessed, said his prayers, and knew the Law.

The Pharisee wore a prayer shawl, a specific head garment, a phylactery (a small leather case containing Scriptures worn around the forehead or left arm during prayer), and fringes upon the borders of his garments. Each of these showed his religiosity, his obedience to Scripture. Because of his exceptional religious acts and his outward pious appearance, he felt he impressed God by the way he lived on earth, and because of the way he lived on earth he was good enough for heaven—both of these positions were personally merited. However, he was not aware that no amount of personal goodness could change his sinful nature—carrion smells putrid no matter how much you douse it with perfume. He was unaware that he stood apart from the grace of God, the very thing he needed most.

Furthermore, the Pharisee's attitude seemed to say, "I have a right to be here because of the distinct contrast from how the publican lived. Publican was the term for those collecting Roman taxes from the Jewish citizenry, and thus considered by the Jews as the basest of sinners. He prayed about himself (some translate this verse to mean "with himself," almost as if he were talking to himself about himself—something self-righteousness tends to do), pointing out his good qualities, versus the publican's bad qualities. His conclusion in talking with himself? "I deserve to be heard because I am better than he." Yet, with all his goodness, he received no audience with the Lord; rather, God rejected his prayer.

Now let's consider the publican.

- He had the favor of the Roman government instead of God, for he was their tax collector.
- He was wealthy in a financially depressed community, but that did not prevent him from extracting taxes from the people.
- He lived in the affluent part of town.

127

- He probably did not attend the local synagogue, nor did he support it financially.
- He may have exacted more tax than the Roman government demanded—that's how publican's got paid.

Still, he approached God in prayer, and was not only heard, but went away justified. Why? How?

The outcome of his prayer was not necessarily about who he was or what he had done. It was about his need of God's mercy. Consider his prayer: "God be merciful to me a sinner." The prayer was short, but it was accepted. Consider what those seven words actually said:

- He was aware of his sinfulness.
- He pleaded for his only hope: God's mercy.
- He didn't compare himself with those more sinful.
- He didn't point out any good thing about himself.
- He didn't make excuses for his sins.
- He recognized his sinfulness compared to a holy God.
- He recognized his hope was in God's mercy alone.
- He realized he had no personal righteousness.

The publican's approach to God was with the right attitude: a sinner needing the Savior. He recognized that his sinful works would cause him to be eternally lost. In contrast, what the Pharisee failed to realize was his good works were insufficient to merit heaven. Good works without grace are like counterfeit money: it looks right, may fool some, but it is of no true value in a legitimate economy.

God didn't show disapproval of the Pharisee's good works; conversely, God looked beyond the works and directly into the heart. That is where the Pharisee lacked: compassion, honesty, humility, love, and repentance. In the chapters to come, I will share Scriptures that reveal our need to produce good works; however, all good works must be balanced with an understanding that salvation was purchased for us by Christ's sacrifice alone, and obedient faith (not acknowledging faith and not good works) applies Christ's death to remit our sins. What should follow salvation? Good works.

I almost forgot to answer my chapter title question, "Can Good Works Save Us?" Only through a miracle of grace! Otherwise, the Pharisee might have gone away justified.

Chapter 11

WHERE DO GOOD WORKS FIT INTO THE

PICTURE

There are too many scriptural references demanding "good works" for us to avoid the subject. But how do good works fit into the message of salvation through grace? Does a message about good works contradict the message of grace? Does the message of grace void the need for good works? Can the message of works be balanced with the message of grace and faith without distorting the doctrine of salvation through grace? I believe there is a biblical balance with the message of grace, faith, and works that pleases God. Further, I believe good works are the result of grace and faith working in our lives. The problem arises when we try to produce grace and faith as a result of good works.

There are multiple opinions in Christendom on the subject of works. Let us consider some of these.

Opinion 1: Good Works Are Not Necessary

This opinion vehemently argues that if we are saved by grace, then good works are not necessary, else Christ's sacrifice alone was insufficient. Further, some argue it is not possible to overcome sin, so why try to be good? This teaching condemns good works as an attempt to "earn salvation," a ploy they say cheapens grace. Since grace cannot be earned (else it would no longer be grace), we should not concern ourselves at all with works. Eat, drink, and be merry because grace has come.

However, this teaching tends to completely omit a host of Scriptures that demand good works—not to earn salvation, but to become and remain an ambassador of grace. Consider such Scriptures:

> Let your light so shine before men, that they may see your good works, and glorify your Father which is in heaven.
>
> Matthew 5:16

> For the Son of man shall come in the glory of his Father with his angels; and then he shall reward every man according to his works.
>
> Matthew 16:27

> But shewed first unto them of Damascus, and at Jerusalem, and throughout all the coasts of Judaea, and then to the Gentiles, that they should repent and turn to God, and do works meet for repentance.
>
> Acts 26:20

> But (which becometh women professing godliness) with good works.
>
> I Timothy 2:10

> Well reported of for good works; if she have brought

up children, if she have lodged strangers, if she have washed the saints' feet, if she have relieved the afflicted, if she have diligently followed every good work.

I Timothy 5:10

That they do good, that they be rich in good works, ready to distribute, willing to communicate. . . .

I Timothy 6:18

That the man of God may be perfect, thoroughly furnished unto all good works.

II Timothy 3:17

In all things shewing thyself a pattern of good works: in doctrine shewing uncorruptness, gravity, sincerity. . . .

Titus 2:7

Who gave himself for us, that he might redeem us from all iniquity, and purify unto himself a peculiar people, zealous of good works.

Titus 2:14

This is a faithful saying, and these things I will that thou affirm constantly, that they which have believed in God might be careful to maintain good works. These things are good and profitable unto men.

Titus 3:8

And let us consider one another to provoke unto love and to good works:

Hebrews 10:24

What doth it profit, my brethren, though a man say he hath faith, and have not works? Can faith save him?

James 2:14

Even so faith, if it hath not works, is dead, being alone. Yea, a man may say, Thou hast faith, and I have works: shew me thy faith without thy works, and I will shew thee my faith by my works.

James 2:17-18

But wilt thou know, O vain man, that faith without works is dead?

James 2:20

Ye see then how that by works a man is justified, and not by faith only.

James 2:24

God gave attention to the works of the seven churches mentioned in Revelation, and they were judged according to their works. At the great judgment, works are a deciding factor, and consider that these being judged are not the church—it seems these are people outside of God's grace, having never experienced His great love, yet they are required to have a measure of good works.

132

And I saw the dead, small and great, stand before God; and the books were opened: and another book was opened, which is the book of life: and the dead were judged out of those things which were written in the books, according to their works. And the sea gave up the dead which were in it; and death and hell delivered up the dead which were in them: and they were judged every man according to their works.

Revelation 20:12-13

Of a truth, we cannot earn God's grace; however, we err when we live as though God's grace expects no effort on our part toward good works. To the contrary, those that have received grace receive an obligation to abound in good works. Further, to de-emphasize works promotes childish irresponsibility, self-centeredness, and apathy in the lives of those professing Christianity; ironically, all of these characteristics are condemned by Scripture. The result of de-emphasizing good works? We have deacons flirting with teenagers, choir members swapping partners, and preachers lusting after their secretaries; again, all condemned by the Scripture—even common sense teaches otherwise. Such is the result of failure to balance works with grace and faith.

Opinion 2: Good Works Are A Prerequisite To Salvation

This second thought tends to suggest that God chooses only qualified good people to be saved, thus elevating works above grace. "Surely no one believes this," we say. Just yesterday I heard abut a minister who told a person praying at the alter to go back to their pew and start living right before they came to the front of the church to pray. Some churches refuse baptism until the convert conforms to a list of rules. This teaching borrows its emphasis from the message of John the Baptist, who commanded Jewish religious leaders to " .. . bring forth therefore fruits meet for repentance" (Matthew 3:8). But I doubt that John advocated grace by works; rather, he challenged those that stood as symbols of Abraham's faith to produce the fruit of Abraham's faith. We have colloquialisms for John's meaning: "Put your money where your mouth is: put up or shut up." Though John denounced the hypocrisy of the religious leaders, he did not promote salvation by works. He promoted salvation through baptism unto repentance. Furthermore, John was the end of the Old Testament prophets, announcing the dawning of a new era of salvation by grace. John well understood the Law was incomplete to bring mankind the salvation sins demanded; therefore, he watched for the appearance of the Lamb of God, and when he saw Him, he immediately pointed his disciples to follow Christ. He accepted the inevitable: his personal ministry's demise due to the conclusion of the age of the Law.

When we consider the idea of good works as a perquisite for salvation, we must consider the teachings of Paul, which tell us the works of the Law could not save us: it took God's grace. In his writings he emphasized the essentiality of salvation by grace.

> Where is boasting then? It is excluded. By what law? of works? Nay: but by the law of faith.
>
> Romans 3:27

> Wherefore? Because they sought it not by faith, but as it were by the works of the law. For they stumbled at that stumbling stone . . .
>
> Romans 9:32

> Knowing that a man is not justified by the works of the law, but by the faith of Jesus Christ, even we have believed in Jesus Christ, that we might be justified by the faith of Christ, and not by the works of the law: for by the works of the law shall no flesh be justified.
>
> Galatians 2:16

> Not of works, lest any man should boast.
>
> Ephesians 2:9

Not by works of righteousness which we have done, but according to his mercy he saved us, by the washing of regeneration, and renewing of the Holy Ghost.

Titus 3:5

I once heard a minister explain that good works have their place in salvation; it's just that some folks get "good works" out of order. "We don't get good to get God; we get God to get good."

Opinion 3: Grace Initiates But Works Complete

A third concept teaches we are initially saved by grace (God's gift), but after the initial experience, it's up to us to live good enough to go to heaven. With this concept my good works keep me saved, therefore I merit heaven by my good works. This concept is akin to the attitude of the religious leaders of Jesus' day (self-righteousness), which Jesus condemned. Why did this attitude receive Christ's vehement disapproval? This concept leaves grace in the past. It is faulty because it fails to realize our goodness is never good enough when compared with the goodness of God, thus, we are on a journey of futility, our good deeds never gaining us the approval for which we strive. "But we are all as an unclean thing, and all our righteousness are as filthy rags; and we all do fade as a leaf; and our iniquities, like the wind, have taken us away" (Isaiah 64:6).

When grace is left in the past, it leaves us spiritually bankrupt when we fail—all will fail. Our failure leaves us in despair, for we cannot simply accept Christ's forgiveness, we have to earn it. Since forgiveness is earned, we work harder to acquire His approval. Guilt motivates us to greater works, but guilt distances us from a relationship with Christ. This distance from Christ creates a vacuum of vulnerability to discouragement, often tempting us to give up on Christianity and return to our old self. Once we succumb to defeat the road back is long and difficult. It is impossible unless we reclaim grace to cover our sins.

While some live in this "work hard at gaining Christ's favor" state, others take a journey of deception, trying to hide their sins from others. Self-righteousness always digresses to hypocrisy—for all will sin, but the self-righteous will try and hide their sin until they work hard enough to regain God's favor. This position isn't necessarily a thought out plan; rather, the individual generally arrives here due to a chain of events. Since salvation is built on personal goodness rather than God's grace, and the individual continues to fall short of what they consider God's expectations—including certain expectations from others—it's either drop out or fake it. The latter seems the lesser of the two evils.

Without the continuing of God's daily grace, when we fall short of God's agenda, we lack the bridge to span the chasm into God's presence—though He hasn't really abandoned us; that's simply our perspective. We have abandoned grace for works. Instead of the work of grace growing us into what God desires, we have relied upon our good works to earn us God's smile of approval. How sinister we sometimes make God. Our good works have failed us: they always do.

Trying to live for God from one of these three concepts, when we fail, where do we turn for hope? It is at this point that we must recognize there is a fourth concept, which I believe is the Bible principle of Christianity. This teaching acknowledges the importance of good works, but does so in light of what the Bible says about grace, faith, and works. Good works cannot save us; still, good works are the result of faith in the grace of God. Furthermore, the concept of salvation through works often does not leave room for failure; rather, it projects a bed of roses Christian walk where the individual is always bigger than the problem, the sick will always be healed, couples are exempt from marital difficulties, and the devil will always take flight at our command. When disappointments and failures come, guilt overwhelms those who have espoused this concept (leaving no room for failure and God's continual work of grace). They question their personal experience of salvation, and often become cynical of Scriptures from which they previously based their "no problem" concept, loosing faith in God and His Word.

Concept 4: Good Works Are A Result Of Grace

We have viewed three concepts that, though with some merit, do not bring a proper biblical balance to the message of grace, faith, and works. There is a fourth concept: Good works is a result of our growing " . . . in grace, and in the knowledge of our Lord and Saviour Jesus Christ. To him be glory both now and for ever . . . " (II Peter 3:18). This is where the Christian must live to remain in a healthy and loving relationship with Christ. This concept does not negate the work of grace (salvation cannot be earned but is the gift of God), nor does it diminish the significance of faith as the activator of grace in our lives. Further, this concept does not overlook the scriptural commands for the believer to manifest a life of good works. Rather, this fourth concept puts each in the right perspective: we no longer try to earn salvation but accept the grace of God to save us. We recognize the necessity of faith for salvation; yet, we do not neglect growth in Christ which produces good works. Consider this analogy as an example of grace, faith, and works in proper balance.

> One late evening a young man walked the darkened country pathway leading to his girlfriend's house. Along the way, he fell into an unsuspected cave-in, of which he tried desperately to get out but could not. By chance, his girlfriend's father came along, and upon hearing the cries for help, lowered a rope into the hole and pulled the young man out. Let's call this grace, for some fathers of a young girl would have left her suitor forever trapped. The next day, the young man went back to the hole with pick and shovel, and filled it up with dirt. Does this earn him the previous grace showed him by his sweetheart's father? No. Does it make him look unappreciative of the grace shown him? No. Does it obligate the father to do something special for him, like giving his daughter's hand in marriage? No. Why should the young man not operate by faith, trusting that he can always avoid the hole in the future? Why didn't he just walk around the hole, leaving it as a reminder of the grace shown him, and if he falls in again, it would be an opportunity for grace to be extended again? He had several options, but he did right by filling in the hole

with dirt, for filling in the hole is the most logical thing to do to avoid falling in the hole again—not to mention removing the potential danger for others if he left the hole open. Likewise, good works (filling in the holes that previously swallowed one up) is the right thing for a person to do once the grace of God rescues him.

Consider the danger for a person who gets save—who previously enjoyed the barroom atmosphere—but fails to fill in the dangerous holes that can swallow up his life: like avoiding the barroom in the future. To continue to frequent the barroom, relying upon God's amazing grace, does not elevate grace: it challenges grace. The logical thing to do is fill in the hole: stop going to the bar. What about the neighborhood grump, always verbally attacking the paperboy, the mailman, and the garbage collector? Should he continue to do so, while proclaiming God's awesome grace? Instead, should he not fill in the hole of grumpiness and replace it with a joyful witness? Furthermore, the real issue is not whether we should or should not produce works, for all produce works. The real issue is what kind of works are we producing: good or bad? Right or wrong? Righteous or unrighteous? Works of the flesh or works of the Spirit? The logical thing for Christians to do is to fill in the holes that formerly engulfed them. And beyond logic, it is the scriptural thing to do.

How do we produce good works without delving into Pharisaism? How do we avoid a self-righteous, hypocritical, judgmental, and harsh spirit? We can produce good works and avoid all these ungodly actions by developing a biblical understanding that includes a balance of grace, faith, and works. Good works are the result of "salvation by grace through faith." Good works are the fruit of the indwelling Holy Spirit. Good works are the ressults of a life growing in God. In contrast, the static Christian—no observable change— is indicative of someone who may have experienced salvation but is not progressing in Christ. Further, evil works are the fruit of a life that either has never experienced grace, or else, denies the Holy Spirit control—by purposeful rebellion or ignorance of God's Word regarding righteous living.

Israel's favored position with God, and the recorded history of that relationship, offers us much insight into this subject. God's grace brought Israel out of Egypt (not their good works toward Him), but after their deliverance from Egyptian bondage, Israel's refusal to allow God control prevented them from entering the Promised Land. Has God changed so that He now offers heaven without any Lordship over our lives? I say no. Consider this warning to the Hebrew Christians in regards to the rebellion of their ancestors:

> Wherefore (as the Holy Ghost saith, Today if ye will hear his voice, harden not your hearts, as in the provocation, in the day of temptation in the wilderness: when your fathers tempted me, proved me, and saw my works forty years. Wherefore I was grieved with that generation, and said, they do alway err in their heart; and they have not known my ways. So I sware in my wrath, they shall not enter into my rest.) Take heed, brethren, lest there be in any of you an evil heart of unbelief, in departing from the living God. But exhort one another daily, while it is called To-day; lest any of you be hardened through the deceitfulness of sin. For we are made partakers of Christ, if we hold the beginning of our confidence stedfast unto the end; While it is said, Today if ye will hear his voice, harden not your hearts, as in the provocation. For some, when they had heard, did provoke; howbeit not all that came out of Egypt by Moses. But with whom was he grieved forty years? Was it not with them that had sinned, whose carcases fell in the wilderness? And to whom sware he that they should not enter into his rest, but to them that believed not? So we see that they could not enter in because of unbelief. Let us therefore fear, lest a promise being left us of entering into his rest, any of you should seem to come short of it. For unto us was the gospel preached, as well as unto them: but the word preached did not profit them, not being mixed with faith in them that heard it. For we which have believed do enter into

rest, as he said, As I have sworn in my wrath, if they shall enter into my rest: although the works were finished from the foundation of the world. For he spake in a certain place of the seventh day on this wise, And God did rest the seventh day from all his works. And in this place again, If they shall enter into my rest. Seeing therefore it remaineth that some must enter therein, and they to whom it was first preached entered not in because of unbelief: Again, he limiteth a certain day, saying in David, Today, after so long a time; as it is said, Today if ye will hear his voice, harden not your hearts. For if Jesus had given them rest, then would he not afterward have spoken of another day. There remaineth therefore a rest to the people of God. For he that is entered into his rest, he also hath ceased from his own works, as God did from his. Let us labour therefore to enter into that rest, lest any man fall after the same example of unbelief.

Hebrews 3:7-19, 4:1,11

Does this sound like "going along for the ride, with no personal effort?" Of course it is significant to point out that the Hebrew Christians were in danger of returning to the works and rituals of the Law in order to obtain salvation, rather than salvation through Christ. The point I want to make is the effort it takes to possess faith. Faith demands action. Faith is evident by our obedience. Look again at some of the commands and warnings of these Scriptures:

- Harden not your hearts, vs 8
- Take heed, lest there be in any of you an evil heart, vs. 12
- But exhort one another, lest any of you be hardened through the deceitfulness of sin, vs. 13
- For we are . . . of Christ, if we hold the beginning . . . unto the end, vs. 14
- Let us therefore fear, lest . . . any of you should seem to come short of it, vs. 1
- Let us labor therefore to enter into that rest, vs. 11

If we ignore God speaking to us, which He does through His Word (through personal reading and also sermons), our hearts can become hardened to His will. In so doing we default to the carnal nature: we grow more desirous of the pleasures of sin, and grow less desirous of the things of God. The disobedient heart can grow to depreciate God's grace. In so doing, we begin a journey that ultimately could end in apostasy: this indefinitely ends one's personal relationship with God's grace.

Apostasy has a starting line and a finish line. Consider these steps that map out the road to apostasy:

- A neglect of the spiritual life through passive living creates room for spiritual apathy; the things of God are not foremost in our lives and are often not taken seriously.
- Unbelief results in failing to take God's Word seriously or in it's entirety, thus much of the teachings of Scripture are rejected or at best neglected.
- The love of the world gains a greater influence than the things of God.
- Since the influence of the world is greater than God's Word (whether rejected or neglected), the deceitfulness of sin and worldly cares develop a tolerance for personal sin.
- Repeated rejection of God's Word produces a hardness of heart, which makes it easier to reject God's warnings, leading to apostasy.

The general truth of the Bible contradicts the popular teaching of eternal security (once one is saved he can never become unsaved). The Bible is full of warnings for those who take salvation lightly. Yet, this is not to earn salvation, which comes by grace through faith, but it is to appreciate the grace of God; further, anything less than the desire for good works is to neglect the grace of God within us. To neglect grace is to try God's patience, and the Bible teaches there is a limit even to God's patience: the flood being a prime example. It is wise to follow the directive of the Apostle, " . . . work out your own salvation with fear and trembling" (Philippians 2:12)? This is not to earn God's grace; rather, it is to appreciate God's grace and to recognize God's love for righteousness and hatred of unrighteousness. With much effort we do those things that God loves, and we abandon those things that displease Him. It is inconceivable that those who truly desire God live passively for Him. We can deduce that those who profess Christianity, but who are unfruitful in good works, are either ignorant of God's Word, or they are rejecting God's Word. God has never overlooked disobedience, and through His written Word He demands and expects obedience, which is a part of spiritual growth.

> For the grace of God that bringeth salvation hath appeared to all men, Teaching us that denying ungodliness and worldly lusts, we should live soberly, righteously and godly, in this present world; Looking for that blessed hope, and the glorious appearing of the great God and our Savior Jesus Christ; Who gave himself for us, that he might redeem us from all iniquity, and purify unto himself a peculiar people, zealous of good works.
>
> Titus 2:11-14

The fruit they bear identifies true believers—good works are the fruit of one saved by the grace of God; conversely, a lack of good works represents something else. If one fails to bear good fruit, the obvious explanation is that the person is not growing in grace and faith, nor in knowledge of the Savior; instead, that person is allowing the old nature to reign. Christ is not Lord of his or her life. Moreover, the devil has a vulnerable prey; furthermore, the prey may eventually become the victim of deception.

Chapter 12

THREE KINDS OF WORKS

No biblically literate person would argue against the need for good works in the Christian life. Yet arguments do arise when we try and balance the subject of works with those of grace and faith, but the three really fit together quite harmoniously. Too often we think of works only in terms of the individual: what one does or does not do. We need to expand our definition of works. From a biblical perspective there are three kinds of works:

- Works of grace: this is the work of Christ to bring us salvation and grow us spiritually.
- Works of righteousness: this is the result of growing in grace and knowledge of Christ; thus, we produce works of righteousness because Christ has saved us and is now resident in our daily lives.
- Works of darkness (unrighteousness): this is the consequence of our fallen nature, our default mode. However, by the grace of God, we stop doing these because Christ has saved us, and grace and faith are now working in us. We are now the children of light, and the Holy Spirit within grants the ability for us to override the default mode of carnality.

A problem arises when we do not properly balance our works with grace and faith. Three ugly words rear up their head and bring confusion, division, and despair: bondage, legalism, self-righteousness. Bondage is the result of trying to earn God's grace by works. Legalism occurs when we produce works out of fear rather than faith. Self-righteousness comes from thinking our works are good enough without the work of grace.

Some confuse the writings of Paul and James, suggesting their teachings were contradictory: Paul promoting the significance of faith, and James promoting the significance of good works. On the contrary, Paul and James believed both faith and good works were a sign of Christian maturity. Though both used Abraham as their primary character (Romans 4, James 2), the seemingly difference of instruction comes because Paul and James were using the term "works" from different perspectives. Consider the difference in meaning:

For Paul, "works" were in reference to the rituals of the Law and were not able to merit salvation because it lacked a Savior. He contended that salvation only came through faith in Jesus Christ. Paul contended with Jewish Christians who insisted certain works of the Law (primarily circumcision and observance of Jewish feasts) were essential for salvation, even though one had experienced the New Birth. Paul's teachings were primarily addressing how one obtained salvation: by grace through faith in Christ's atoning death.

James primarily addressed works as a sign of Christian maturity: how one ought to live after they were saved. His use of the term "works" was in reference to the Christian's duty of obedience to the commands of Scripture after salvation. James contended that good works are evidence one has truly experienced salvation through the grace of God.

Both Paul and James taught that true saving faith produced works of righteousness. However, Paul wanted to emphasize to the early Christians that salvation was through faith in Christ and not in the Old Testament works of the Law; further, Paul emphasized that Abraham was justified by faith rather than by how righteous he lived. His life wasn't perfect, evident when he persuaded Sarah to shade the truth. Further, Abraham tried to help God fulfill the promise by caving to Sarah's plan for him to father a child by her handmaid. Paul emphasized Abraham's salvation—justification—came by his faith in God, which was evident by his willingness to sacrifice his son. The emphasis was on his faith, not the works that were a result of his faith. Even though Isaac was the tangible means by which God's promises to him were to be fulfilled, Abraham believed somehow God would fulfill His promise even if he obeyed God's directive to sacrifice Isaac (Genesis 22:2). Notice again, the emphasis by Paul was Abraham's faith, not his works. Using the same Bible character, James proceeded to persuade the early Christians that good works were evidence of faith. Since faith produces good works, therefore they are inseparable, he focused on good works as being the evidence of faith. If there are no good works, we can conclude that faith is lacking.

When Abraham was challenged by the Lord, he didn't just talk about faith, nor passively believe; rather, Abraham obeyed (faith at work). He left his homeland, he followed God's leading, he believed God for a son in his old age, and he was willing to sacrifice that son of his old age. Since faith and works go together (if you have faith you will have works), James was able to say, "Ye see then how that by works a man is justified, and not by faith only" (James 2:24). Take away good works and you are operating in disobedience, which is contrary to the law of faith. Take away faith and your works are dead, for they do not glorify Jesus Christ. James taught, let's quit merely talking about faith and start living a faithful life. Good works are the result of living according to the faith that is in our hearts. This is not promoting good works as a means of salvation; rather, it is promoting good works as a result of salvation.

When we consider the manner in which Paul and James wrote of man acquiring God's righteousness, we recognize they spoke from two concepts. One, righteousness is something that is given to us. It has nothing to do with our being good; rather, it comes to us at the New Birth as God's gift. God takes from us our cloak of unrighteousness, and He replaces the old garment with His cloak of righteousness. This imparted righteousness is something God does for us because of His faithfulness to His promises. "Not by works of righteousness which we have done, but according to his mercy he saved us, by the washing of regeneration, and renewing of the Holy Ghost" (Titus 3:5). At the New Birth, God removes our unrighteousness, and before we have done one good deed, He imparts His righteousness within us. One moment we are a sinner, and the next moment we are righteous before God. It is not so much a state of doing; it is a state of being. Christ makes us righteous.

James references a second concept of righteousness, which he calls imputed righteousness; namely, God takes note of the manner in which we live after we come into a relationship with Him. For Abraham, he acquired a heart of obedient faith. He believed God; therefore, he acted upon his faith. James emphasized Abraham's obedience. This is what James referenced when he spoke of the imperativeness of good works. "And the scripture was fulfilled which saith, Abraham believed God, and it was imputed unto him for righteousness: and he was called the Friend of God. Ye see then how that by works a man is justified, and not by faith only" (James 2:23-24). James insisted that true faith produces good works; further, he insisted that God expects us to produce good works, and these are credited to us by the Lord for righteousness—right living. How? Isn't our righteousness pitiful in God's sight? True, but the difference is that we produce good works out of our faith in the grace made possible through Christ's atoning death. When considering our good works of faith, the emphasis is still on Christ's atoning sacrifice. When His sacrifice is applied to our works, though they may be miniscule when compared to His righteousness, Christ applies His righteousness to our efforts. This righteousness is God working through us (the Spirit within producing His continual righteousness), not us being good apart from God's grace. Both faith and works—not one in front of the other, but each working in harmony with the other—are possible when we appropriate God's grace through faith in His Word to all that we do.

To fully comprehend Paul's argument regarding righteousness through faith, we must realize he was establishing the means of salvation as being through Christ alone, not the deeds of the Law. But Paul likewise insisted that the believer produce good works. Bible Commentator Donald C. Stamps offers tremendous insight regarding righteous living when he elaborates on Paul's writings in Romans: "I beseech you therefore, brethren, by the mercies of God, that ye present your bodies a living sacrifice, holy, acceptable unto God, which is your reasonable service. And be not conformed to this world: but be ye transformed by the renewing of your mind, that ye may prove what is that good, and acceptable, and perfect, will of God" (12:1-2).

> Believers must possess a single-minded passion to please God in love, devotion, praise, and holiness, and to offer the members of their bodies for His service. Our greatest desire and prayer should be to live a life of holiness and to be accepted by God. This requires separating ourselves from the world and drawing ever nearer to God. We must live for God, worship Him, obey Him, take His side against sin, stand for righteousness, resist and hate evil, perform works of kindness for others, imitate Christ, follow Him, serve Him, walk after the Holy Spirit, and be filled with the Spirit. We must present our bodies to God as dead to sin and as the temple of the Holy Spirit. Paul implies several things in this verse. We must realize that the present world system is evil and under the rule of Satan.

> We must stand against the prevailing and popular forms of the spirit of this world, proclaiming instead the eternal truths and righteous standards of God's Word for Christ's sake.

> We must despise and abhor what is evil, love what is righteous and refuse to yield to the various types of worldliness that constantly surround the church, such as greed, selfishness, humanistic thinking, political maneuvering for power, envy, hate, revenge, impurity, filthy language, ungodly entertainment, sensuality, immodesty, immorality, drugs, alcohol, and worldly companions.

> We must have our minds conformed to God's way of thinking by reading and meditating on His Word. We must have our plans, goals, and ambitions determined by heavenly and eternal truths, not by this evil, temporal, and transient age.[1]

Jesus harmonized both Paul's and James' concept of righteousness when He spoke to the adulterous woman: "Neither do I condemn thee: go, and sin no more" (John 8:11). He instantaneously gave to her a clean slate: righteousness. But he commanded of her to live a righteousness lifestyle. She had to have faith that He truly did not condemn her; she had to make some decisions about how she should live. What a balance Jesus gave! Grace and good works pivoted on faith. How can anyone challenge Him?

Chapter 13

GRACIOUS LIVING

We are not only to be recipients of grace; we are to dispense grace. As one hand is extended towards God to receive of His goodness, the other should be extended toward our fellowman, reflecting the grace God has given to us. This is the grace of God active within our lives—the work of the indwelling Holy Spirit—resulting in good works. Consider this scripture:

> Let no corrupt communication proceed out of your mouth, but that which is good to the use of edifying, that it may minister grace unto the hearers. And grieve not the holy Spirit of God, whereby ye are sealed unto the day of redemption. Let all bitterness, and wrath, and anger and clamour, and evil speaking, be put away from you, with all malice: And be ye kind one to another, even as God for Christ's sake hath forgiven you.
>
> Ephesians 4:29-32

149

Though there is an immediate change that comes with salvation, many changes do not automatically happen; rather, we change as we better understand God's Word, His will, and His ways. Still, some changes take tremendous effort. Chuck Swindoll, writing on the subject of *Graciously Disagreeing and Pressing On*, offers this insight:

> One of the marks of maturity is the ability to disagree without becoming disagreeable. It takes grace. In fact, handling disagreements with tact is one of the crowning achievements of grace.
>
> Unfortunately, the older we get the more brittle we become in our reactions, the more tedious and stubborn and fragile. For some strange reason, this is especially true among evangelical Christians. You would think that the church would be the one place where we could find tolerance, tact, plenty of room for disagreement, and open discussion. Not so! It is a rare delight to come across those in the family of God who have grown old in grace as well as in knowledge.[1]

Graceful living takes effort. Note the writing of Paul to his young associate Titus. The book is not very long, so I suggest you read the entire three chapters. Paul did not say grace prevents bitterness and loud evil speaking towards others, nor does grace always automatically manifest kindness and forgiveness. Though God's grace brings the capacity to do these things (for we are new creatures in Christ Jesus), effort must come from within the individual, and change is still a choice; thus, we produce good works by much effort. The letter to Titus contains multiple instructions on making the effort to live righteous. Paul reminds Titus of how we obtained salvation, but he is quick to point out that the new-found Christian life is responsible to produce good works:

> Not by works of righteousness which we have done, but according to his mercy he saved us, by the wash-

ing of regeneration, and renewing of the Holy Ghost;
Which he shed on us abundantly through Jesus
Christ our Saviour; That being justified by his grace,
we should be made heirs according to the hope of
eternal life. This is a faithful saying, and these things
I will that thou affirm constantly, that they which
have believed in God might be careful to maintain
good works. These things are good and profitable
unto men.

Titus 3:5-8

Stephen R. Covey, in his number one national bestseller *The
7 Habits of Highly Effective People*, shares a very moving story of
Victor Frankl, a prisoner in the death camps of Nazi Germany.

Frankl was also a psychiatrist and a Jew. He was im-
prisoned in the death camps of Nazi Germany, where
he experienced things that were so repugnant to our
sense of decency that we shudder to even repeat them.

His parents, his brother, and his wife died in the
camps or were sent to the gas ovens. Except for his
sister, his entire family perished. Frankl himself
suffered torture and innumerable indignities, never
knowing from one moment to the next if his path
would lead to the ovens or if he would be among the
"saved" who would remove the bodies or shovel out
the ashes of those so fated.

One day, naked and alone in a small room, he began
to become aware of what he later called "the last of
the human freedoms"—the freedom his Nazi cap-
tors could not take away. They could control his entire environment, they could do what they wanted to
his body, but Viktor Frankl himself was a self-aware
being who could look as an observer at his very in-
volvement. His basic identity was intact. He could
decide within himself how all of this was going to

affect him. Between what happened to him, or the stimulus, and his response to it, was his freedom or power to choose that response."[2]

If under such horrible conditions one could choose a response, there is no excuse for the Spirit empowered Christian to live apart from extending the grace of God through gracious living. We can choose our response to others.

Extending good works toward others is a command of Scripture: a directive which comes with the power of the Spirit to perform. We are to render kindness and forgiveness, not because this is easy to do, nor because the New Birth makes it an automatic response; rather, we are to be kind and forgive because it is the Christian (Christ-like) thing to do: " . . . even as God for Christ's sake hath forgiven you" (Ephesians 4:32). This sometimes takes great effort and is in contrast to our carnal default mode. All the while, we understand we are not doing such in an effort to earn salvation; we are simply obeying the Savior. Good works are not works "for" salvation; rather, they are works "because" of salvation. They are not works to earn God's favor; rather, they are works to express gratitude for God's favor extended to us. They are not works to impress God; rather, they are works of obedience to the one who suffered for our sins. They are not works to prove our goodness; rather, they are works to please the one we love. They are not works to manipulate God; rather, they are works to manifest the purpose of God. They are not works to earn God's love; rather, they are works of extending God's love to others.

Too often we extend grace only to the gracious—a reciprocal process—, but Jesus challenged this when he asked, "Do not even the publicans the same?" Jesus continued, "And if ye salute your brethren only, what do ye more than others? do not even the publicans so? Be ye therefore perfect, even as your Father which is in heaven is perfect" (Matthew 5:46-48).

A publican, or tax collector in Jesus' day, epitomized the most ungracious of humans, for he had no mercy as he collected taxes, profiting often by overcharging. Yet, the publican knew how to be gracious to his friends. Does this act of friendship make him one to be respected by the widow lady whose grocery money he just took? Of course not! And God certainly doesn't look favorable to the publican just because he was nice to his friends. Likewise, the Lord does not reward us for being kind to those who are kind to us, for such a response takes little effort. Too often this is the limit to our graciousness: a scratching each other's back concept. Yet we seem to find ways to justify speaking harshly to those who cross us, disagree with us, criticize us, or just plainly dislike us. However, the grace of God not only gives us the wherewithal to extend grace, it demands that we extend grace, both to those who love us and to those who hate us. As the goodness of God led us to repentance, likewise, our goodness to those who do not merit a kind word (at least from our perspective) is a witness of the grace of God in our lives. Hurtful words, rude actions, and hateful attitudes are never appropriate in the Holy Spirit controlled life: graciousness is always in order. But you argue, "I only gave them what they deserve." What if Jesus Christ had that attitude at the crucifixion? None of us would be saved. The "eye-for-an-eye" mentality of the Law was to show the awfulness of sin, mankind's sinful state, and his need of a Savior. Once the Savior came, He gave us a new law: love even your enemy. This shows the awesomeness of God's love, the redeemed state of mankind, and the power of the indwelling Christ. Consider Paul's instruction to Titus on the subject of being gracious:

> Put them in mind to be subject to principalities and powers, to obey magistrates, to be ready to every good work, To speak evil of no man, to be no brawlers, but gentle, shewing all meekness unto all men. For we ourselves also were sometimes foolish, disobedient, deceived, serving divers lusts and pleasures, living in malice and envy, hateful, and hating one another.

> Titus 3:1-3

Titus was Paul's faithful assistant in the gospel. Paul's testimony won him to Christ (Titus 1:4), and he became a co-worker with Paul. One such occasion of their missionary endeavors was establishing the gospel in Crete, an island nation southeast of Greece in the Mediterranean Sea. Upon leaving the island, Paul entrusted Titus with remaining in Crete and continuing the Christian work. Paul later sent this letter to him, offering instruction in areas of qualifications for elders, dealing with false teachers, and the proper roles of church members. Interestingly, Paul emphasized the necessity of good works as the product of a faithful Christian life. The Cretans had a reputation of being ungracious in their words and actions. He quotes one of their own: "One of themselves, even a prophet of their own, said, the Cretians are alway liars, evil beasts, slow bellies" (Titus 1:12). Matthew Henry explained:

> " . . . they were infamous for falsehood and lying; to play the Cretan, or to lie, is the same; and they were compared to evil beasts for their sly hurtfulness and savage nature, and called slow bellies for their laziness and sensuality, more inclined to eat than to work and live by some honest employment."[3]

Crete was an island country with its own reputation, and that not a good one. I view them as lounging all day, waiting for a ship to come by, full of people whom they could swindle. Yet, Paul wrote to Titus that, even the Cretans, once touched by the grace of God, have the capacity to show forth the character and purpose of Jesus Christ through the manifestation of their good works. These are Paul's instructions:

> For the grace of God that bringeth salvation hath appeared to all men, Teaching us that denying ungodliness and worldly lusts, we should live soberly, righteously, and godly, in this present world; Looking for that blessed hope, and the glorious appearing of the great God and our Saviour Jesus Christ; Who gave himself for us, that he might redeem us from all iniquity, and purify unto himself a peculiar people, zealous of good works.
>
> Titus 2:11-14

When it comes to extending God's grace through good works, no one is excluded: not for personality, background, circumstances, nor favor. The Cretans were not exempt, no matter how bad their culture. Paul emphasized the necessity of good works as being the fruit of a converted heart, controlled by the Holy Spirit. The Christian is not to use culture as an excuse; moreover, we're called to become a counter-culture of hope. In his letter to Titus, Paul reminded him four times of the responsibility for gracious living: "In all things showing thyself a pattern of good works" (2:7); "zealous of good works" (2:14); "to be ready to every good work" (3:1); "be careful to maintain good works" (3:8). If the Cretans were not exempt, even though their social reputation was far removed from the "beatitudes" of basic Christianity, why do we file for exemption when it comes to treating our fellowman with graciousness? Exemption request denied! Our culture doesn't get a free pass.

What do we mean by "gracious living"? Perhaps these two accounts can help us put a handle on the subject.

I've been associated with two ministers who come to mind when I think of gracious living. One was a model of graciousness, for he lived by the "turn the other cheek" message of Christ; the other was the opposite, for he leaned toward the "eye-for-an-eye" concept of the Law. Both ministers were pastors, and both had encounters with cantankerous neighbors. The first had a neighbor who threw trash on the church property. This kind pastor graciously picked up the trash and said nothing. I'd want to say this pastor's kindness so impressed the neighbor that he came to church, ran to the altar, and gave his life to God. Sorry, it didn't happen that way; instead, the man threw more garbage on the church property, trying to agitate the minister into a confrontation. The minister continued to graciously pick up the garbage and say nothing. This went on for weeks. Finally, the garbage dumping ceased, and the man became a friend, even helping the pastor to purchase additional property for the church. Gracious living! Returning good for evil. Praying for those that despitefully use you and persecute you. Loving your enemy. Sound familiar? This is the teaching of our Lord about gracious living.

Now to the other minister and his neighbor. A cherry tree was on the church property— about three inches on the church property. One beautiful summer day, a neighbor's small children crossed the three inches onto the church property and stole a few of the cherries: cherries that the pastor's wife was going to use to bake a pie. Bad neighbors! The pastor scolded the children and chased them away from the church property with instructions for future activities, especially regarding the cherries. That day, the neighbors became enemies of the church for life. A few days later, black birds converged upon the tree and ate all the cherries: so much for a cherry pie. A more gracious approach has no guarantees, but it does raise the odds, and it certainly is biblical. Solomon warned, " . . . a brother offended is harder to be won than a strong city . . . " (Proverbs 18:19). The responsibility for the extension of grace rests with the Christian, not the unbeliever.

We must not think that gracious living will have immediate results in the lives of all we encounter. This is also true of people you deal with in church: sometimes the opposite is true. There are those who interpret kindness as a weakness, using it to their advantage to barrel over their subjects. Not everyone will like you. In fact, no matter how kind you are to some people, they will not respond positively to your graciousness, but this must not prevent you from continuing to spread kindness everywhere you go. Let me share one last thought that may encourage you along your journey of gracious living.

I vividly recall an account in my life where graciousness paid off, but it took years to see any results. A parishioner had terribly misjudged my motives. His harsh and erroneous criticism caused me much personal pain. For years I lived with the accusations he had made, and because of the circumstances, I had little if any opportunity to defend myself. During those years I never retaliated, nor did I speak harshly to others about him, while he openly vented his anger against me. My kindness to him showed little if any positive results; however, I continued to do so, though I must admit that I felt all seemed hopeless. During a very difficult time in his life, I went to him. Others were there, so I nervously waited to speak with him. When my turn came, he arose from his chair, extended one hand to mine and placed his other hand on my shoulder. To my surprise he tearfully expressed, "Please forgive me for what I've felt and said against you." I was shown firsthand how the graciousness of God, through me, had won a brother offended.

True, there are times for confrontation. Paul told Titus to "rebuke with all authority" (Titus 2:15), but confrontations need to be done with love. Gracious living may not get the results you desire today, but it leaves the door open for a later opportunity.

Chapter 14

PAUL'S MESSAGE TO THE ROMANS

Paul never intended for his grand message on grace and faith to be used as a weapon to destroy the corresponding message of good works; otherwise, Paul would need to apologize to the church at Corinth. Paul spoke very little to the Corinthians regarding grace, but he constantly scolded them for their works of unrighteousness and lack of good works. If we are to fully comprehend Paul's message to the Corinthians, we must recognize from other writings that he believed in a balance of grace, faith, and works. To lean too heavily in any one direction is to veer from God's plan. Even after experiencing the New Birth, some Jewish Christians leaned too heavily toward the works of the Law; in so doing they caused some dissension within the segregated church (Jew and Gentile). Paul guided the Roman church around the entrapment of salvation through the works of the Law by urging them to understand salvation cannot be earned; it comes by grace through faith. Yet, he didn't neglect the significance of aspiring to works of righteousness, and he concludes his message by an appeal to good works: a biblical balance! One author gives this pictorial word description:

The famous capital city was rife with activity. It is no wonder that the apostle to the Gentiles longed to visit this hub of the empire, a city on seven hills. Rome, with its youthful and insane emperor, Nero, and its promiscuous society, was also a very religious city. With Rome adopting the various religions of the world, Paul is anxious to infiltrate the gospel of Christ from the servants' quarters to the Imperial residence. As he is anxious, he is of equal caution, to keep the religions of the world out of Christianity. He cannot wait another year, actually, it will be three, and so he sends a letter as a substitute and prelude to his trip, to the church at Rome. "Rome, the city of marble", boasted Augustus. Probably no other city in the world felt any more the effects of Christianity, yet Christianity suffered the pains of death in this city more than any other.

It is here that Christians wrapped in the skins of animals would be fed to hungry dogs. It is in this city that burning Christians would serve as torches to offer light for special events. Even today you can still visit the catacombs, underground tunnels in which Christians hid, worshipped, died and were buried.

To this city of over one million population, one half of them slaves, Paul longed to visit. He did not know that he would arrive in chains nor that it would cost him his life. But he did know the "good news" that he brought with him and its power to bring salvation. Today, the Empire is but history, yet Christianity still thrives. And Paul's message to the Roman Christians is quoted by millions, yet understood by too few.[1]

In the beginning of his letter to the Roman church, Paul quotes from the Old Testament prophet: " . . . the just shall live by faith" (Habakkuk 2:4). Thus, Paul begins the subject of salvation as being justification by faith and not works, though he does not soften the message against sin. The reason for their terrible sin is revealed in verse 21: "Because that, when they knew God, they glorified him not as God, neither were thankful; but became vain in their imaginations, and their foolish heart was darkened." How did the Gentile world know God prior to the giving of the Law? This is explained in verse 20. There is a universal light that all mankind can clearly see: the light of creation. The true God was not beyond discovery by the sincere heart. Where there is a creation, there must be a creator. Evolution is an age-old problem; Paul confronted it in his first century writings to the church at Rome. Man refused to accept the simple truth that God created the world and all that existed.

The battle over creation still exists in our courts today. Have you ever wondered why scientists, who insist on proof for everything else, accept as the means of creation such an explanation so unscientific as evolution? The reason? If God created mankind, then we are in subjection to Him and must someday give an account to Him for our life; conversely, if man can push from his mind the thoughts of a creator God, then he does not have to answer to anyone but himself. The downward spiral begins. His carnal nature succumbs to Satan and sin, and he becomes vain in his own imagination, and his foolish heart is darkened. This is not only a twenty-first century problem; it has long existed. The Psalmist of old elaborated regarding the process, "The fool hath said in his heart there is no God" (Psalm 53:1). Paul further explains the depths of sin into which the foolish heart enters:

> Wherefore God also gave them up to uncleanness through the lusts of their own hearts, to dishonour their own bodies between themselves: For this cause God gave them up unto vile affections: for even their women did change the natural use into that which is against nature: And even as they did not like to retain God in their knowledge, God gave them over to a reprobate mind, to do those things which are not convenient . . .

> Romans 1:24,26,28

The Scriptures explain that when God quit interrupting mankind's thoughts, they defaulted to the basest of evil thoughts—without conscience mankind free-falls into corruption. This is why unbelievable cruelties happen daily in our society. Man can do the worst of sin and not feel guilty. And yet the person living in the heart of the jungle—with no Bible in his native tongue but recognizes God as Creator—may live by principles better than some who live in a Christian nation but reject God as Creator. Uncivilized societies will condemn many a civilized people who over time rationalize God from their society.

We have already determined from Scripture the first basis for coming to God is that of faith. " . . . for he that cometh to God must believe that he is . . . " (Hebrews 11:6). Even if man never hears the truth of the Bible, there is a natural conviction—a Divinely created moral bearing—placed in his heart by the Creator. This natural conviction causes society to produce laws against stealing, cheating, lying, murdering, and immorality. Most societies experience some form of moral conviction. This is true for most of us as individuals. When we break these natural laws, the heart smites us and we feel our guilt and need of forgiveness. The Gentiles, however, had rejected the natural laws of God for so long that they were without controls in their lives. After years of rejecting God's natural laws, they became desensitized to morality and imparted the same to the succeeding generation. Eventually, "God gave them over to a reprobate mind" (Romans 1:28). God let them live without His internal law nagging at their hearts; consequently, their own ideas, without godly convictions, controlled their every decision. Paul expresses the downward course of destruction, which the Gentiles had followed:

> For this cause God gave them up unto vile affections: for even their women did change the natural use into that which is against nature: And likewise also the men, leaving the natural use of the woman, burned in their lust one toward another; men with men working that which is unseemly, and receiving in themselves that recompence of their error which was meet. And even as they did not like to retain God in their knowledge, God gave them over to a repro-

bate mind, to do those things which are not convenient; Being filled with all unrighteousness, fornication, wickedness, covetousness, maliciousness; full of envy, murder, debate, deceit, malignity; whisperers, Backbiters, haters of God, despiteful, proud, boasters, inventors of evil things, disobedient to parents, Without understanding, covenantbreakers, without natural affection, implacable, unmerciful: Who knowing the judgment of God, that they which commit such things are worthy of death, not only do the same, but have pleasure in them that do them.

Romans 1:26-32

Evil, however, is never satisfied. The Gentiles relied on their own wisdom apart from the wisdom of God. Man's wisdom, however, is insufficient. Our nature is to sin. Someone once expressed the wisdom of man accordingly:

> You can know all about geology, but if you don't know the Rock of Ages, you don't know anything. You can know all about botany, but if you don't know the Rose of Sharon and the Lily of the Valley, you don't know anything. You can know all about astronomy, but if you don't know the Bright and Morning Star, you don't know anything. You can know all about masonry, but if you don't know the Chief Cornerstone, you don't know anything. You can know all about literature, but if you don't know the story of an old crimson cross, you don't know anything.[2]

Thus, Paul's greatest task in reaching the Gentile world was to resurrect a sense of moral estrangement. He did this by teaching that this singular God of Old Testament Scripture was the only true God. This God was manifest in flesh through Jesus Christ and died for the sins of the world. Christ offers salvation to all who accept the gospel. Unless they follow this one true God and his commandments, the Gentile world would continue its downward plunge into sin. A society cannot get better without God. Societies cannot be good because of secular education; conversely, a godless society will continue to digress, and over time, it will follow the path taken by all godless societies of the past.

To the Jews, Peter said repent (Acts 2:38). To the Gentiles, Paul said believe (Acts 16:31). What is the difference between repentance and believing? Were they preaching a contradictory message? No. The apostles personalized the message. The Jews already believed in the Creator God, but they rejected him as the Messiah. They must repent of their evil deeds and acknowledge that Christ was God. The Gentiles however, had many gods; so Paul taught they must believe in the only true God, the true Creator God, the only God that can save—the God of the Old Testament. They had to turn from all other gods and believe in this One. Paul's message: "Forsake all idols and return to the worship of the Creator God of Genesis." The apostles'—Peter and Paul—messages were not contradictory; to the contrary, they addressed the primary problem of the Jews and the Gentiles, which contained a unique difference. Though both needed forgiveness from their sins, the approach to accomplish this varied accordingly.

In chapters two and three of the letter to the Roman church, Paul explained the need of a Savior by all, for sin is universal. Since the sin of Adam and Eve, all came under the curse of sin, and God cast mankind from His presence. Because of his sinful nature, his separation from God is perilous, for he had no means to reconnect with God. To better explain the predicament of man, think of an astronaut walking in space. He is held onto the spaceship by a line, but for some unexpected reason, the line snaps. He is now floating freely in space. The spacecraft is a different weight, and thus they travel at different and separating speeds. He struggles to reach the spacecraft but cannot. He is hopelessly doomed. Thus was the predicament of man with God: adrift and traveling in a different direction than God. Not only could man not bridge the gap caused by his sinful nature, but his sinful nature was not inclined to do the things pleasing to God. Mankind had a multi-fold problem:

- Adam's sin caused him and his descendants to lose fellowship with God.
- Mankind lacked the ability to bridge the gap that separated

him from God.

- Even if he wanted to do right, his sinful nature compelled him to do wrong.

In chapter three of Romans we understand that the Law did not change a man's sinful nature; rather, it condemned him for his sinful acts. His nature was to sin, and the Law pointed out the error of these sinful acts. Even though the Law told mankind how to live, it did not supply inner strength to obey the rules it contained; moreover, when mankind sinned, the Law acted as a judge to condemn, not a lawyer to defend. Though mankind constantly brought sin offerings according to The Law, the sacrifices never relieved his guilt of sin. Moreover, the writer of the Book of Hebrews explains that a man's sin remained with him under the Law.

> For the law having a shadow of good things to come, and not the very image of the things, can never with those sacrifices which they offered year by year continually make the comers thereunto perfect. For then would they not have ceased to be offered? because that the worshippers once purged should have had no more conscience of sins. But in those sacrifices there is a remembrance again made of sins every year. For it is not possible that the blood of bulls and of goats should take away sins.
>
> Hebrews 10:1-4

After the Old Testament sacrifice, one still remained with a feeling of guilt. Paul explained, that if the Law was sufficient, there would have been a release of the guilt, and there would have been no need for Jesus Christ's death. The Law, however, was insufficient to remove the sin—thus the condemnation remained. Jesus Christ, however, was sufficient to pay the debt created by sin, to remove the sin, and to remove the condemnation brought on by the sin. Therefore, we must not reach backwards to something that is inferior. The works of the Law served a purpose, but it didn't work to reverse the curse of sin prior to Calvary, nor did it work after Calvary.

In chapter four of Romans, Paul points out that Abraham obtained the righteousness of God because of his faith, not because of his good works. Abraham lived approximately five hundred years before the Law was given to Moses at Mount Sinai; still, Abraham obtained righteousness without the Law. Paul uses this as an argument against the teaching that one had to observe the rituals of the Law to obtain righteousness.

The question then arises, "How did Abraham obtain righteousness before Calvary?" Some Jewish Christians in Rome taught if you were not of the seed of Abraham by birth, you would have to become so by, not only experiencing the New Birth of Christianity, but also by adhering to the law of circumcision and observing certain feasts of the Law. In chapter four of Romans, Paul explains that Abraham's righteousness did not come because of the covenant of circumcision (which he did observe even before the Law), but because of his faith. Faith in what? It was faith in God's character, God's goodness, and that God would be true to the promises He made. Abraham manifest this faith before God introduced to him the covenant of circumcision:

> But to him that worketh not, but believeth on him that justifieth the ungodly, his faith is counted for righteousness.
>
> Cometh this blessedness then upon the circumcision only, or upon the uncircumcision also? for we say that faith was reckoned to Abraham for righteousness.
>
> And he received the sign of circumcision, a seal of the righteousness of the faith which he had yet being uncircumcised: that he might be the father of all them that believe, though they be not circumcised; that righteousness might be imputed unto them also:
>
> And the father of circumcision to them who are not of the circumcision only, but who also walk in the steps of that faith of our father Abraham, which he had being yet uncircumcised.

> For the promise, that he should be the heir of the world, was not to Abraham, or to his seed, through the law, but through the righteousness of faith.
>
> Romans 4:5, 9, 11, 12, 13

Paul points out that Abraham, though a hundred years old, still believed that God would give him a son by Sarah. "He staggered not at the promise of God through unbelief; but was strong in faith, giving glory to God; And being fully persuaded that, what he had promised, he was able also to perform" (Romans 4:21).

This man of faith, Abraham, lived two thousand years before Calvary, yet he was considered righteous as we are considered righteous. How could one who lived before Calvary obtain righteousness? How could one who lived before the Apostles preached the message of salvation have their sins forgiven? There is something very beautiful about Calvary that we often overlook: Calvary's blood flowed backward to the Old Testament believers. Consider, it would have been unfair for those born before Calvary if there was no means for their salvation. Yet, the writer of Hebrews pointed out that it was impossible for the blood of bulls and goats to remit their sins. How then can they that lived before Calvary be saved? It began with faith. Realize the significance of faith; faith is the prerequisite of salvation. "But without faith it is impossible to please him: for he that cometh to God must believe that he is, and that he is a rewarder of them that diligently seek him" (Hebrews 11:6). To enact salvation one must act upon their faith. We have previously described this as saving faith; it is faith in action based upon the commands of Scripture. Paul explains the necessity of God's Word:

> For after that in the wisdom of God the world by wisdom knew not God, it pleased God by the foolishness of preaching to save them that believe.
>
> I Corinthians 1:21

For whosoever shall call upon the name of the Lord shall be saved. How then shall they call on him in whom they have not believed? and how shall they believe in him of whom they have not heard? and how shall they hear without a preacher? And how shall they preach, except they be sent? as it is written, How beautiful are the feet of them that preach the gospel of peace, and bring glad tidings of good things! But they have not all obeyed the gospel. For Esaias saith, Lord, who hath believed our report? So then faith cometh by hearing, and hearing by the word of God

Romans 10:13-17

The Gentile nations, however, had rejected this faith Paul preached. They carved and named their own gods, or else worshipped a part of the creation (sun, moon, stars, rain, rivers), instead of the Creator. Because of their lack of faith in the Creator God, God himself gave them up to believe the wicked imaginations of their hearts. The Gentiles became stooped in sin. Now, after almost four thousand years of the burden of sin, Paul preached to them about a Savior God who was the Creator God. However, to merely acknowledge that you believe in this God was not enough. To be saved, they had to progress into a deeper faith. This faith comes by hearing the Word of God: believing that God can save you, and acting upon God's plan of salvation.

Hebrews chapter eleven is called the "Heroes of Faith" chapter. Notice there is something unique about these exemplary Bible characters; each acted upon their faith:

- By faith Abel offered a sacrifice.
- By faith Enoch pleased God.
- By faith Noah prepared an ark.
- By faith Abraham obeyed God.

Saving faith draws us into obedience to the Word of God. To say "I have faith" or "I believe" or "I accept Christ" is but to acknowledge God and His Word. We must take the step of obedience to His Word. Jesus told His disciples to do more than have believers recite a sinners' prayer. He demanded baptism, but also discipleship: "Teaching them to observe all things whatsoever I have commanded you" (Matthew 28:20).

We have expressed how we are to respond to God regarding salvation, but how then can anyone before Calvary be saved? It had to do with their faith toward God. Those who are regarded to have obtained salvation under the Old Testament possessed an obedient faith, and because of this faith, God dealt with them in light of future Calvary—the sacrifice which was to come. Mount Calvary is the focal point of all history. Like the cliché, "all roads lead to Rome," something even more impressive is that all roads of salvation lead to Calvary—past, present, future. Those that lived before Calvary will be judged according to their obedience to their knowledge of God; the road they journeyed was likewise a road that led toward Calvary, and Calvary's blood flowed backwards to meet them.

The crucifixion was a singular event that took place approximately 29 A.D.; however, the blood of Christ flows both forward and backward. Today we obtain salvation, also through faith, but faith in Jesus Christ's atoning blood—the blood flowed forward to meet us.

Those that lived before Calvary obtained salvation because of their faith, which moved them to obey God, whether it was their conscience speaking to them, adherence to the Law, or submitting to the voice of a prophet. Today, we receive salvation through obedience to God's Word, and this is more than acknowledging that Christ died for us; it is allowing the Savior to become Lord of our lives.

Consider from this analogy the role that "works" play in salvation. Firemen arrive at the scene of a terrible fire. They quickly spot a woman standing at a window on the second floor. She is screaming, "Can you save me?" They reply, "Yes, we can save you. Trust us and do what we tell you." They carry a net over to the house. Standing under the window they yell to her, "Jump." She replies, "Save me, can you save me?" They say, "Yes, we can save you. Jump into the net." She replies, "I'm afraid." They quickly put a ladder up to the second floor. By this time the downstairs is completely engulfed in flames. Time is of essence. A fireman, risking his life, climbs up the ladder. At the top he explains to the woman, "I can save you. Follow me back down the ladder." She draws back in fear, "Save me," she screams. The fireman reaches for her. She pushes him backwards. He struggles to catch himself. All the while the woman screams, "Save me." Smoke has filled the room. The fireman pleads with her. He reaches her an oxygen mask. She brushes it aside. Flames leap up through the floor. The floor collapses. The woman falls to her death, but note, the fireman is under no obligation to give his life. He did all he could do, with every means available. Yet she refused to cooperate, even though he had sufficient means to save her. And if she had cooperated, all the credit for her salvation would have gone to the fireman; however, he could not save her because of her failure to work with him.

Such is the grace of God. He has made provision for our salvation. He can save us! He gave his life to pay the debt of our sins. A means for us to receive this unmerited favor has been provided. He, however, will not force salvation upon us. We recognize it as grace, but we must accept it by obedient faith; therefore, you cannot disassociate works from obedient faith.

Works are important!

To contend that one is saved by simply believing, but should not strive to be a better person, is contrary to the following scriptural references:

Matthew 5:16; 25:35-36; 26:7-10; I Thessalonians 1:3; I Timothy 6:18; Revelation 2:2; Hebrews 10:24; 13:16; Psalm 34:14; 37:3, 27; James 2:17-18; Luke 6:35; I Peter 2:12-15; 3:11; Romans 13:3; Galatians 6:10; Nehemiah 13:14; Acts 9:36; James 4:17; Titus 2:7-14; 3:8

However, there is no contention with the teaching that our works cannot merit salvation. That is clear from a hosts of Scriptures, many which we have already shared: Matthew 7:22-23; Romans 3:20; Galatians 2:16; Ephesians 2:8-9; Titus 3:4-5.

To fully grasp what Paul believed, we must study his entire letter to the Romans. Chapter twelve sheds light on the significance of Christian works and gives a balance to Paul's teachings regarding grace, faith, and works. Up to this point, Paul has been very careful to point out that salvation is by grace. Remission of one's sins is impossible to do personally: this is the work of Christ. The stain of sin cannot be removed by deeds of man. Salvation cannot be earned or merited; it is free to those that will believe and receive the work of Christ at Calvary.

Perhaps the reason Paul expressed so fervently "salvation by grace" is because some Jewish Christians insisted the Old Testament law of circumcision, along with other Jewish rites, were absolutes for salvation. Paul stressed that the grace of God is above the Law. The Law was merely our schoolmaster to bring us to Christ. The Law was a type, a pattern or an example of that which was to come—Christ and Calvary. That which was to come, Christ, had to come in order for the Law to be effective in the past, for the Law, with all its different sacrifices, still lacked a sacrifice that could remove sin.

Paul used eleven chapters to teach the grace of God. In the twelfth chapter he does not contradict what he had already written, but he added to the first eleven chapters the duties of a Christian. The New Birth creates a new man, for the old man—with all the sinful deeds of the past—has passed away. The past is behind; however, the new man must now walk in new light.

Thus, Paul writes:

> I beseech you therefore, brethren, by the mercies of God, that ye present your bodies a living sacrifice, holy, acceptable unto God, which is your reasonable service. And be not conformed to this world: but be ye transformed by the renewing of your mind, that ye may prove what is that good, and acceptable, and perfect, will of God.
>
> Romans 12:1-2

Beseech, from the Greek "parakalo," means to beg or plead. Since you have been partakers of this heavenly gift, it is only right that you present your bodies:

- A living sacrifice—Christ wants our life dedicated to Him rather than self.
- Holy—pertaining to freedom from impurities of the flesh by means of the indwelling Holy Spirit transforming the individual into that which pleases Christ.

169

- Acceptable unto God—well pleasing unto God in contrast to conforming to the world.

Paul describes these qualities as being our reasonable service, especially since we have received such a wonderful salvation. He tells the believers they should not follow (be not conformed) after the example of the world, but they should be changed, that they might please God. How? "By the renewing of the mind." The indwelling Spirit of Christ brings a change of lifestyle for the Christian. The change takes place first in the heart; subsequently, the changed heart affects our thought pattern. This renewed mind dictates a new life-style to the believer. To be called Christian is a misnomer for anyone who exhibits no change. To be like Christ is to be separated and unique from the world. The cross that Christ called us to bear is not an ornament worn around the neck. For Paul, cross bearing represented his neck on a chopping block. Even martyrdom did not save him—salvation is the work of Calvary—, but martyrdom certainly reflected a balance of grace, faith, and works in his life.

Chapter 15

LIVING ABOVE SIN

Some interpret Paul's message to the Roman church as suggesting that living above sin is impossible; therefore, any effort on our part to do so is futile. So, don't worry about trying to be good; rather, be happy while you sin, for God understands and is delighted to accommodate sin with His abundant grace. God does have an abundance of grace, but Paul never intended for his message to be interpreted with such looseness. To the contrary, Paul taught that a victorious Christian life was possible and should be pursued. In considering his message to the Roman Christians, we need to consider "the three R's of sin:"

The three R's of sin:
- Reason (cause) of sin.
- Result of sin.
- Remedy for sin.

The reason of sin is disobedience. Adam and Eve were given one rule to live by: don't eat of one particular tree. It was their disobedience to this command that brought the knowledge of sin and a nature that defaulted to sin (pleasure seeking, self serving), which we call the fallen nature.

We cannot truly imagine the ugliness of sin as viewed by God. The result of sin was that all born into the human race would have the nature of Adam—even nature became affected adversely by the curse of God because of sin. First, mankind was cast out of the presence of God. Fellowship with God was broken (spiritual death). Second, all mankind would be born impure as God regards purity. Third, the earth was no longer a utopia, for man was cast out of the Eden paradise; consequently, life became full of toil for mere survival. Fourth, man's life span on earth was cut short. He would eventually die a natural death—through the years that lifespan has gone from many hundreds of years to less than a hundred. Finally, all mankind will someday be resurrected and judged according to his deeds; he will be eternally rewarded or sentenced to eternal punishment.

The remedy for sin, however, is the grace of God. This grace, made possible through the shed blood of Jesus Christ, is offered to all mankind. Saving faith in Christ's atoning sacrifice is sufficient to remit one's sins, and the indwelling Spirit, along with the Bible, is adequate to keep the individual in continual fellowship with Christ.

A marvel of New Testament salvation is the process by which it is obtained. When sin broke our communion with God, man became totally hopeless to reclaim fellowship with God. He did not possess the ability to remove his transgressions of sin; therefore, he could never enter into God's holy presence. Neither could he eliminate the control that sin had over his life. Since God alone can remit sin, man could not save himself. Salvation was eternally out of his reach, but God had a plan for redemption before he placed man in Eden. Literature has many love stories, but none can compare to the love story of redemption.

The redemption plan slowly unfolded as God visited selected individuals for various reasons. Though God is a Spirit and thus invisible, He appeared in various forms in the Old Testament. This temporary appearance of God is called a theophany, but unlike mankind, it was not flesh. It could not experience pain, hunger, or death. The appearance of a theophany in Scripture is somewhat difficult to differentiate from an angel. With close examination of Scripture, we recognize some of these heavenly visitations was God in a temporary, visible, and humanlike form. One of the most notable appearances of a theophany was the appearance of three men—angels—unto Abraham, who recognized them as heavenly messengers. Abraham specifically communed with one that he called the judge of all the earth (Genesis 18)—believed to be God. The theophany of the Old Testament was a typology of the New Testament Incarnation—God made flesh. Paul offers a description of Christ as the God/man: "And without controversy great is the mystery of godliness: God was manifest in the flesh, justified in the Spirit, seen of angels, preached unto the Gentiles, believed on in the world, received up into glory" (I Timothy 3:16). Jesus Christ was God Incarnate—God in human form. He came to earth to specifically purchase man's redemption. Christ was different than the Old Testament theophany in that He was both divine and human. As a man He became tired and fell asleep in a sailboat on the Sea of Galilee; as God He rebuked the storm that threatened to engulf the boat. As a man he became hungry and plucked grain from the field to satisfy that hunger; as God He multiplied the loaves and fish to feed the thousands. He brought the dead back to life during His ministry, than suffered and died at the hands of the angry mob and Roman soldiers. The mystery of salvation was that Christ was not conceived of mortal man; He was conceived of the Spirit of God. His flesh was therefore sinless, untainted by the bloodline of Adam. For approximately thirty-three years He lived completely free of sin, and He died being perfect; subsequently, He became the perfect sacrifice. At Calvary, He took upon himself the cloak of man's unrighteousness. From the first sin of Adam, to the present, and into the future, Christ took upon Himself the sins of the world. He suffered, in man's place, the judgment of the sins of mankind. No wonder his flesh cried out " . . . my God, my God, why hast thou forsaken me?" (Matthew 27:46). He felt the burden and judgment of the sins of all mankind. The Spirit of God did not intervene; therefore, His flesh felt the full impact of the judgment of sin. It was the flesh of God that hung suspended between heaven and earth. He drank from the cup of wrath that we might drink from the cup of salvation.

By the sin of one man—Adam—all mankind came under the condemnation of sin; therefore, all must die. By the death of one man—Jesus Christ—all have opportunity for that death to apply to their sins; therefore, all have opportunity for eternal life. Man is born with a sinful nature, and it is natural for him to sin. He sins because he is a sinner. A dog does not become a dog because he chases rabbits; he chases rabbits because he is a dog. Likewise, we sin because it is our nature. This is our natural birth, but Jesus Christ offers a second birth, a spiritual birth. At this birth we are given the nature of Christ to offset our carnal nature; therefore, we can live above sin, for our new nature counteracts the power of the carnal.

Since we have the nature of Christ, it is right for us to live righteously. We are not born again because we live right, but we live right because we are born again. We do not have to continually succumb to sin. We can conquer sin that previously dominated us. Some try to excuse sin instead of overcoming it. Some suggest God's grace is like a flowing river that even though we continually throw litter into it, the river continues to flow pure, washing away the debris. We must understand, however, that over a period of time, even a clear river may become full of rubbish and therefore contaminated. Such is the Christian life that persists in sin. That person will become spiritually unfruitful. Jesus said the tree that does not bear fruit must eventually be cut down. This is not to say that we will never sin, but we must not deliberately sin with the thought that Jesus delights in automatically taking care of sin; conversely, we should strive to overcome sin through God's grace.

The phenomenon of the New Birth experience is that we now desire to please God rather than follow sin. Christ's Spirit in our lives gives us strength to overcome temptation; however, we must be aware that we are in a spiritual warfare. When we are born again, the fruit of the flesh—lying, cheating, cursing, smoking, drinking, fornicating—is replaced by the fruit of the Spirit— love, joy, peace, longsuffering, gentleness, goodness, faith, meekness, and temperance. But the enemy doesn't concede defeat; rather, it lurks nearby, waiting for an opportunity to invade and reclaim.

Consider the example of an island, polluted by the litter of careless inhabitants. A hurricane sweeps across the island and washes away the debris, leaving the island pristine. But an unchanged lifestyle by the inhabitants will eventually render the island undesirable again. Further, unless the inhabitants create a plan of prevention, the debris washed out to sea may eventually return to pollute the sandy beaches. Such is our life: polluted by sin until Christ comes in and the water of baptism washes away the pollution of sin. Remember, the former sins get tired of treading water or camping out, and they will attempt to come back home. This becomes a continual spiritual warfare. We keep them out by reliance on the indwelling Christ, and we strengthen the inner man through spiritual disciplines: prayer, fasting, Bible reading, worship, Christian fellowship, and consistent church attendance. Some may argue this is trying to earn salvation by works, but this is not the case. These are no longer works of the flesh, but they are the works of Christ within us—continual grace and active faith. That is why we have nothing to boast of save Jesus Christ within.

It is impossible to live a life pleasing to God without the New Birth experience. Paul explains the significance of this experience, for as sinners we are spiritually dead but alive to sin. The New Birth reverses the order; we become dead to sin and alive in Christ. How? Through partaking of the death, burial, and resurrection of Christ. We need to realize the following comparison of Christ's death, burial, and resurrection to the New Birth experience of which we can partake:

The Experience of Christ	Our Experience in Christ
Death: crucified by the Roman government	Repentance: death to the old nature
Burial: placed in a borrowed tomb	Baptism: His death applies to our sins
Resurrection: victorious over death	Holy Spirit infilling: victorious living

The grace of God is not a license for us to sin, but it offers a plan whereby we can be forgiven our sins and overcome the world, fleshly lust, and the devil. For us to continually sin does not cause grace to be magnified but shows an absence of appreciation, deficiency of dedication, and a shortage of spiritual maturity. Since sin was the product of the old nature, righteousness should become the product of the new nature. " . . . even so now yield your members servants to righteousness unto holiness" (Romans 6:19). In this verse, "now" refers to after we have been born again. It is therefore imperative that we experience a born again conversion. The New Birth is essential for living a victorious life.

Chapter seven of Romans is one of the most misinterpreted chapters in the Bible. Consider these verses:

> For we know that the law is spiritual: but I am carnal, sold under sin. For that which I do I allow not: for what I would, that do I not; but what I hate, that do I. If then I do that which I would not, I consent unto the law that it is good. Now then it is no more I that do it, but sin that dwelleth in me. For I know that in me (that is, in my flesh,) dwelleth no good thing: for to will is present with me; but how to perform that which is good I find not. For the good that I would I do not: but the evil which I would not, that I do. Now if I do that I would not, it is no more I that do it, but sin that dwelleth in me. I find then a law, that, when I would do good, evil is present with me.
>
> Romans 7:14-21

Many use these verses as a license to sin, while others use them to establish the message of eternal security or "once saved, always saved." It is also used to substantiate the doctrine of purgatory: that even Christians must still experience a time of purification after death until worthy to enter into heaven. All of these, however, are misconceptions of the true meaning of these verses. In this chapter, Paul paints a picture of the struggle that goes on in a man's life when he tries to live for God under the Law of the Old Covenant, instead of experiencing New Testament salvation. Paul points out that the Law causes us to realize we are sinners and in need of some greater force to combat sin within our lives.

> What shall we say then? Is the law sin? God forbid. Nay, I had not known sin, but by the law: for I had not known lust, except the law had said, Thou shalt not covet. But sin, taking occasion by the command-

ment, wrought in me all manner of concupiscence. For without the law sin was dead. For I was alive without the law once: but when the commandment came, sin revived, and I died.

Romans 7:7-9

Paul was not disappointed that the Law pointed out his sinful state, but he realized the Law was incomplete in that condemnation with no means of justification is sheer torture. The chapter continues to express the inner struggle of trying to obey the Law of God with a nature that was contrary to the Law of God. He concludes with: "Oh wretched man that I am! Who shall deliver me from the body of this death?" (Romans 7:24). He seemed so desperate. His mind wanted to serve God, but his flesh desired the things of the world. The Law only reached the mind; it did not change a person's nature. Under the Law, man was left with a two-fold problem: His sins remained with him; his desire for sin remained with him. Life was a vicious cycle of failures, guilt, sacrifice, and lingering guilt. Even if he could change his desire, he still had his past sins hanging over his head. Or, if he could get rid of his sins, the desire to sin was so strong, and his resistance so weak, that he would eventually fall back into sin. He desired to learn the Law of God, but the more he knew about God, the more condemnation he felt. But the Law was no accident, nor was it a cheap shot at man from a disappointed God. Paul also expressed, "Wherefore the law was our schoolmaster to bring us unto Christ . . . " (Galatians 3:24). First, note that he references the Law in the past tense: it was our schoolmaster. As a schoolmaster, what does the Law teach us? All have sinned and come short of God's glory. Unless we experience the New Birth we will continue to sin. But the schoolmaster could only teach; he could not produce change regarding our sinful state. The Law did what it was designed to do: bring us to Christ. What does the Law not do? It does not cleanse us from our sins, nor give us power to overcome sin. It does not change our nature, thus our desire for sin is still present. The Law lacked a perfect and life changing sacrifice for sin. The Law lacked Christ and Calvary, but it pointed us toward them, and it worked temporarily only because Christ and Calvary were coming.

177

The Bible was not originally divided into chapters and verses; this was done much later so the readers could reference the writings more conveniently. Bible translators saw a need for a uniform way of locating a specific verse, thus, the division of chapter and verse came about. The first edition of the New Testament to appear with a division of chapter and verse was published in 1551. This division is accredited to Henry Stephens. It soon gained universal acceptance. Though this division is very helpful, it can sometimes cause us to isolate and thus incorrectly interpret Scripture. This is true of Romans chapter seven. It is often used to prove that living above sin is impossible. "Sin a little every day" is man's mantra from chapter seven. We must realize, however, that Romans chapter seven is incomplete without Romans chapter eight. In chapter seven, Paul expresses what it was like to try and live for God under the Law, before his Christian conversion. The Law only made him conscious of his sins; it did not give him the inner strength to overcome. To better understand chapter seven, think of the Book of Romans as one lengthy and continuous letter, so chapter eight is a continuation of chapter seven. The answer to Paul's question of "Who shall deliver me?" is given in the last verse of chapter seven: "I thank God through Jesus Christ our Lord. So then with the mind I myself serve the law of God; but with the flesh the law of sin" (Romans 7:25). But chapter eight gives us a detailed explanation of how Christ delivers us.

We should note that in chapter seven the word "I" is used thirty-eight times in twenty-five verses. In contrast, it is interesting that in chapter eight Paul uses the personal pronoun "I" only twice, but he references "Spirit" twenty-one times. Paul refers to the gloom and despair of defeat experienced under the Law as being corrected by the indwelling Spirit of Christ who grants a victorious life. Paul points out eight results of a Spirit filled life:

- Verse 10: The old body (old nature) is dead (subdued).
- Verse 10: The new nature (the righteousness of God) now lives by the grace of Christ.
- Verse 11: Resurrection power is resident in the believer.
- Verse 13: We can now mortify (overcome by spiritual disciplines) the flesh.
- Verse 14-15: We are the Sons of God by adoption through the New Birth.

- Verse 17: We are heirs of eternal glory.
- Verse 28: Divine protection is given us.
- Verses 37-39: We are more than conquerors through Christ that lives in us.

Wow! What a change when we rely upon the Spirit instead of our own power. Under the Law, it is man trying to live for God by obeying 613 laws (365 of them negative); conversely, under grace, it is God living in man, with two commands to obey that fulfill the entire Old Covenant requirements: love God and love your fellow man. Under the Law, it is man working for God; under grace, it is God working through man.

In Romans seven, "I" equals struggle and failure. Paul found that works without grace and faith are futile. In chapter eight he finds victorious living through Christ. This experience was impossible under the Law, but it was made possible through the New Birth experience. If something can be biblically classified as sin, or even leaning in the direction of sin, the Christian has the power to overcome sin by the indwelling power of the Spirit. With this promise we should strive to overcome sin, not ignore or excuse it. This is the true Bible message, but if we fail, where does that leave us? We still have faith in God's grace! And that's why it's so amazing.

Some Personal Thoughts

The more I study the Scripture regarding works of righteousness, the more inadequate and unworthy of heaven I feel. It is then that I call upon the Lord in faith, desiring that the work of grace grow me beyond my failures and into the Christian He wants me to become. I quote Scriptures regarding His love and mercy, and I sense His grace again in my life. Through His Word He extends to me His fellowship and offers assurance of eternal life. I accept these through faith. His grace beckons me onward into a greater knowledge of His Word and into continual communion with Him. Once in His presence I realize His challenge to "be holy," to "do more," to "stretch," to "produce fruit," to "change my lifestyle," and to "submit to His Word." I again see my haggard humanity, but this is not an endless merry-go-round of futility. It is an exhilarating balancing act of following the Scripture; it is a tedious journey across the tight rope of the Christian life. Am I discouraged? No. Confused about where I stand with God? No! For when I sense fear gripping my heart, I steady myself with the balancing bar of faith, and I look below for assurance of His love. The safety net of grace is still there. I take another step. I can make it! And so can you!

Endnotes

Chapter One - The Right Choice

1) Jerry Bridges, The Discipline of Grace, (Colorado Springs, CO: NavPress, 1994), pages 12-13

Chapter Two - Grace Examined

1) Jerry Bridges, The Discipline of Grace, (Colorado Springs, CO: NavPress, 1994), pages 36-37

Chapter Three - What Grace Doesn't Do

1) J.I. Packer, Knowing God (Downers Grove, IL: Inter Varsity Press, page 163)

2) Donald C. Stamps, The Full Life Study Bible (Grand Rapids, MI: Zondervan, 1992) page 1752

3) Packer, page 158

4) Packer, page 160

5) Packer, page 151

6) Packer, page 152

7) Packer, page 153

Chapter Five - Whatever Happened To The Law

1) Martin Abegg, Title Page (Biblical Archaeological Review, Nov/Dec 1994) page 53

2) Kathleen Parker, Article, Have We No Standards, (The Indianapolis Star, August 3, 2013)

Chapter Six - How Am I To Live Under Grace

1) Donald C. Stamps, The Full Life Study Bible (Grand Rapids, MI: Zondervan, 1992) Stamps, page 1839

2) Stamps, page 1885

Chapter Seven - What Is Faith

1) The New Webster's Dictionary, (Danbury, CT: Lexicon Publications, Inc., 1993) page 144

2) Matthew Henry's Commentary, (Revel, Volume VI) page 938

3) Henry, page 938

Chapter Nine - Evidence Of Faith

1) William Ernest Henley, 1849-1903

2) Bruce Larson, Living Out The Book of Acts (Dallas, TX: Word Publishing, 1984) page 155

3) Larson, pages 158

4) Larson, pages 160

5) Bernard Koerselman, What The Bible Says About Saving Faith (Chandler, AZ: Berean Publishers, 1992) pages 164-165

Chapter Twelve - Three Kinds Of Works

1) Donald C. Stamps, The Full Life Study Bible (Grand Rapids, MI: Zondervan, 1992) Stamps, page 1753

Chapter Thirteen - Gracious Living

1) Charles R. Swindoll, The Grace Awakening (Dallas, TX: Word Publishing, 1990) page 173

2) Stephen R. Covey - The 7 Habits of Highly Effective People (NY, NY: Simon & Schuster, 1989) page 69

3) Matthew Henry's Commentary, (Revel, Volume VI) Henry, page 859

Chapter Fourteen - Paul's Message To The Romans

1) Author wishes to give credit for this quote but has failed to determine the source.

2) Source unknown to author